T.E. LAWRENCE'S IRISH ANCESTRY AND RELATIONSHIP TO SIR WALTER RALEIGH

by

Ronald D. Knight

Printed by LITHOPRESS, Caroline Place, Weymouth Dorset DT4 8NW.
Tel: 01305 760780 sales@lithopress.co.uk

To my wife Iris, who has had to endure hours, days, and weeks of trailing around various research establishments, and innumerable locations, in pursuit of any detail however obscure and tenuous, in connection with the Chapman family story - especially of T.E.Lawrence.

Also by the Author:

THOMAS HARDY O.M. AND SIR EDMUND GOSSE LITT.D.
(First edition 1968; second revised edition 1978)
HAMBLEDON'S CRICKET GLORY Series: Volumes 2-19 & 26-27
(1974 - continuing)
THE KNIGHT FAMILY 'JOURNAL' (Quarterly)
(1979-1986 discontinued)
COLONEL T. E. LAWRENCE (Lawrence of Arabia) VISITS MR. & MRS. THOMAS HARDY (1985)
T. E. LAWRENCE AND THE MAX GATE CIRCLE
(First edition 1988; second revised edition 1995)
T. E. LAWRENCE: HIS ORDERS, DECORATIONS AND MEDALS (1989)
THE HOME FRONT Life in Dorset 1939-1944 (An Evacuee's Experience) 1999

Published by the author:
Ronald D. Knight
339 Dorchester Road
Redlands, Weymouth
Dorset DT3 5AT

ISBN: 0 903769 91 3

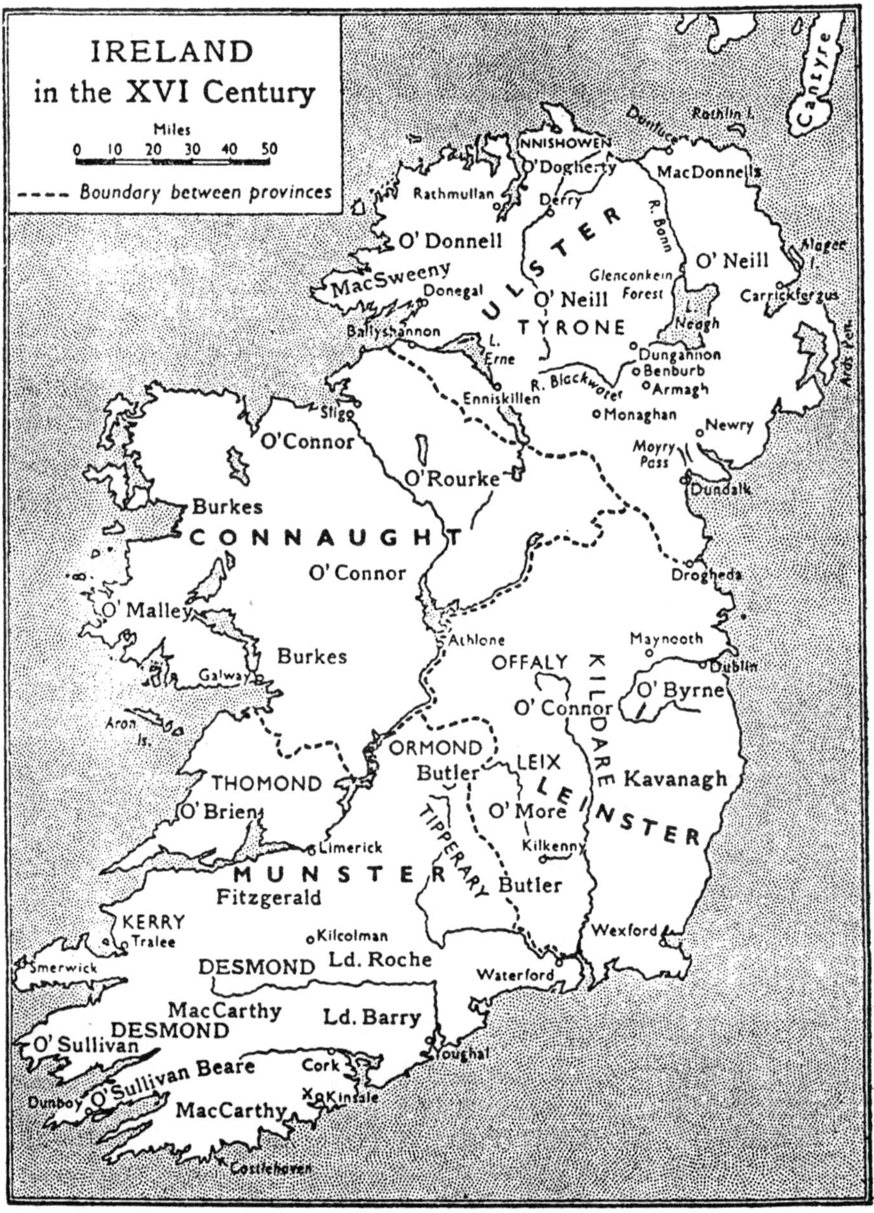
IRELAND
in the XVI Century
Miles
0 10 20 30 40 50
Boundary between provinces
INNISHOWEN
O'Dogherty
Rathlin I.
Cantyre
Dunluce
MacDonnells
Rathmullan
Derry
R. Bann
O'Donnell
ULSTER
O'Neill
Magee I.
MacSweeny
Glenconkein Forest
Donegal
O'Neill
TYRONE
Carrickfergus
L. Neagh
Ballyshannon
L. Erne
Dungannon
Benburb
Armagh
R. Blackwater
Enniskillen
Ards Pen.
Sligo
Monaghan
Newry
O'Connor
Moyry Pass
O'Rourke
Dundalk
Burkes
CONNAUGHT
O'Connor
Drogheda
O'Malley
Athlone
Maynooth
Burkes
OFFALY
KILDARE
Dublin
Galway
O'Connor
O'Byrne
Aran Is.
ORMOND
Butler
LEIX
THOMOND
LEINSTER
Kavanagh
O'Brien
TIPPERARY
O'More
Limerick
Kilkenny
MUNSTER
Butler
Fitzgerald
KERRY
Tralee
Kilcolman
Wexford
Smerwick
DESMOND
Ld. Roche
Waterford
MacCarthy
Ld. Barry
DESMOND
O'Sullivan
Youghal
O'Sullivan Beare
Cork
Kinsale
Dunboy
MacCarthy
Castlehaven

CONTENTS

ILLUSTRATIONS

ACKNOWLEDGEMENTS

Acknowledgements are made to authors of the many printed sources used (most of which are listed in the Bibliography), persons consulted, and other assistance received, including: David Champernowne; Alan Chapman; Clifford Chapman; Stanley H. Chapman; Steve Chapman; Cork City Local Studies Library; Cork County Library, Cork; Michael Culloty; Peter Day, Keeper of Collections at Chatsworth House, Derbyshire; Devon Record Office, and Westcountry Studies Library, Exeter; Dingle Local Studies Library, Dingle; Dorset County Museum, Dorchester; Cora Fox; Galway County Local Studies Library, Galway; John Gavin; M.A.Higgins; Irish Family History Society, Naas, co. Kildare; the Library of the Irish Genealogical Research Society, % The Irish Club, London; Kerry County Council Local Studies Library, Tralee; Kerry County Museum, Tralee; Leicestershire & Rutland Family History Society; Leicestershire County Record Office, Leicester; Nancy Lenihan; Michael MacCarthy Morrogh; National Archives of Ireland, Dublin; National Library of Ireland, Dublin; Robert Noel, Bluemantle Pursuivant of the College of Arms, London; Tom Reilly; County Roscommon Heritage & Genealogy Company; Roscommon County Library, Roscommon; the Sisters of Charity of Jesus and Mary, Delvin, co. Westmeath; Wexford County Reference Library, Wexford; Witt Library, Courtauld Institute of Art, London. Also all those many other persons whose names are generally unknown, but who kindly gave directions and information regarding sites, locations, etc.

DICTIONARY OF TERMS

APPURTENANCE - A thing that belongs to another, a "belonging"; a minor property, right, or privilege, belonging to another more important, and passing in possession with it; an appendage.

BARONY - In Ireland a division of a county: equivalent to an English 'hundred'.

BURGAGE - A tenure whereby lands or tenements in cities and towns were held of the king or other lord, for a certain yearly rent.

CARRUCATE or **CARUCATE** - A measure of land, varying with the nature of the soil, etc., being as much as could be tilled with one plough (with its team of 8 oxen) in a year; a plough-land.

CONCEALMENTS - Ancient royal lands occupied without lease or grant during the Irish wars; lands held by lessees or their descendants although the lease had expired; lands legally forfeit upon attainder or through suicide but hidden and detained from the Crown; lands improperly held from the Crown through technical flaws in the lease or grant, etc.

DEMESNE - Possession (of real estate) as one's own, i.e. in one's own hands as possessor by free tenure.

ESCHEAT - An 'incident' of feudal law, whereby a fief (territory held in fee) reverted to the lord when the tenant died without leaving a successor qualified to inherit under the orignal grant. Hence the lapsing of land to the Crown, or to the lord of the manor, on the death of the owner intestate without heirs.

FIANT - A warrant addressed to the Irish Chancery for a grant under the Great Seal. Found in the formula *fiant literæ patentes* ('let letters patent be made out') with which these documents formerly commenced.

IMPROPRIATOR - A lay-person in possession of a church living or benefice; or of its revenues, specially associated with tithes, particularly since the Reformation.

MESSUAGE - The portion of land intended to be occupied, or actually occupied, as a site for a dwelling-house and its appurtenances.

PLOUGHLAND - See **CARRUCATE.**
RECTORY - A rector is a parson or incumbent whose tithes are not impropriate. Also applied to the holders of ancient chapelries and perpetual curacies. Thus a rectory is a benefice held by a rector. A lay rector is a layman receiving the rectorial tithes, or in whom the rectory is vested.
SEIGNORY - Feudal lordship or dominion; the authority, rights, and privileges of a feudal lord. The territory under the dominion of a lord.
TENEMENT - Land or real property which is held of another by any tenure; a holding. A building or house to dwell in; a dwelling-place, a habitation, residence, abode. A portion of a house tenanted as a separate dwelling; a flat; a suite of apartments, or even a single room so let or occupied.
TRICHA-CED or **CANTRED** or **TROKAHID** - Equivalent to a **BARONY.**

ABBREVIATIONS

CEC *The Champernowne Family* by C. E. Champernowne, 1953.
CSPI Calendar of State Papers for Ireland - PRO.
IGI *International Genealogical Index.*
NLI National Library of Ireland, Dublin.
PRO Public Record Office, Kew.
PROI Public Record Office of Ireland (now National Archives of Ireland), Dublin.

PREFACE

This is another of those Lawrence projects which I had decided to undertake, in mid-1997, as being one not apparently tackled to any determined conclusion. The intention is to prove, or at least substantiate or otherwise, the allegation of there being a 16th century family connection between that of Sir Walter Ralegh and the Chapman ancestors of T. E. Lawrence. Also, to ascertain the history, details, and of extent of the Irish property supposedly granted to the Chapmans in the late 16th century. Finally, how did the Chapman fortunes rise over the centuries, and finally fall in the 20th century?

At the T. E. Lawrence Society's Symposium in 1998 I said that this research project was actively on-going, though I did seem to be going round in circles. But happily I had had the impression that they were not concentric circles, but rather one long spiral. Thus I would either hopefully come to a *super nova* in due course - or else disappear into some black hole!

There have as a result been two enjoyable visits to the Republic of Ireland, during which related researches were undertaken, as well as many ex-Chapman properties as possible located and photographed.

What I now present is the result of three years' detection endeavours. For this to a certain extent takes the form of a detective story, where clues have to be followed up, and evidence sifted, substantiated, and proved - or discarded. First enquiries made were generally depressingly negative, but soon some surprising information came to light. Some readers may not accept the final conclusions drawn, which do not appear to agree wholeheartedly with what was generally, and even fondly, believed. I make no apologies in advance for this, but pass on the torch for others to disprove, discredit, - or more hopefully further substantiate and improve on my researches for this thesis.

Previous publications of mine have also been the obvious products of a non-academic amateur - without benefit of grants, publishing advances, or other financial support -

especially needful when much of research material may be in a foreign country, albeit just across the Irish Sea. To order and borrow books from libraries is getting increasingly more expensive, especially when obtained from out of county. Hopefully it is thought to have served some useful purpose.

In mitigation I cannot do more than quote from a 1960s ground-breaking researcher and publisher in the cricketing sphere, the late Rowland Bowen. Cricket in the 18th century is another study interest of mine; and although the following quotation from Bowen thus concerns cricket, it could equally apply to the basic subject of this thesis - the biographical study into T. E. Lawrence:

Nature abhors a vacuum and that, perhaps, is why fools rush in where angels fear to tread. It now appears that there is a very real and pressing need for a publication to deal with the more serious aspects of cricket's past as well as to re-chronicle, as a matter of record, some of the more interesting and worth-while facts about cricket below its top levels.

It has always been a feature of cricket writing, apart from topical events, that the best, as well as the most valuable research has been produced by those who regard it as a hobby, and who have wide-ranging other interests; by the amateur in the best eighteenth century sense of the term. If Ashley-Cooper [in the early 1900s] was an exception in these, since he relied on his writings for his living, yet his approach was that of the scholar, not of the day-to-day writer for the popular newspapers. In this modern age, what is now needed is a Nuffield Chair of Cricket History and Research, but till that is founded, there are plenty of people up and down the country who have something worth while to say, and we believe, to read...

Then, something that many writers will associate with:

And further, by these, my son, be admonished; of making many books there is no end; and much study is a weariness of the flesh.

(*Ecclesiastes*, chapter 12, verse 12.)

Ronald D. Knight, Weymouth July 2000

THE PERCEIVED EARLY CHAPMAN FAMILY ANCESTRY

It may firstly be opportune to remind those readers who may not be quite aware of just what T. E. Lawrence's connection was with the Chapman family of Ireland. Lawrence's father had been born in 1846 as Thomas Robert Tighe Chapman, at South Hill, Delvin, co. Westmeath. In 1873 he married Edith Sarah Hamilton Boyd. Whilst living at Clanhugh, near Mullingar, co. Westmeath, they had four daughters. Thomas Chapman lived on his private means, which permitted of comfort, but not luxury. In 1885 he ran away with the family governess, Sarah Junner/Maden, and they adopted the name LAWRENCE. Thomas was not able to obtain a divorce, and thus his and Sarah's subsequent five sons were all illegitimate. Their second son was Thomas Edward, the future famous 'Lawrence of Arabia'. (See Chapter 10 for further details.)

Thus starting with the basic concept, what to date has been the perceived and accepted Chapman family's early ancestry?

Editions of *Burke's Landed Gentry* for the past 100 years or more have consistently said:

The parent stock of this family flourished through several generations, in and near the town of Hinckley, co. Leicester. The branch settled in Ireland was established there by John Chapman and his brother William, under the auspices [= patronage *Oxford Dictionary*] of their cousin-german, Sir Walter Raleigh, through whose influence John obtained grants of lands in the co. Kerry, which, on the fall of his patron, he was obliged from pecuniary difficulties, to dispose of to the 1st Earl of Cork, receiving in return the large sum, in those days, of £26,400. He lived eight years after this transaction, leaving at his decease, his brother, William Chapman,

Most biographies of Lawrence which touch on his ancestry seem to have been uncritically based on these statements.

What did Lawrence himself have to say about his early ancestry? His first published mention seems to have been in a letter dated 14 January 1926, in reply to D. G. Hogarth's request as to what to put in an article on Lawrence commissioned by the *Encyclopædia Britannica*:

Encyc. Brit. Yes by all means. Let me try my hand...(*The red ink is not for publication*).
"L's family, though (*Leicestershire*) not >Irish in origin, had been settled for some while (*Queen Elizabeth*) near Dublin (*60 miles N.W.*) His only recent ancestor (*since Sir W. Raleigh*)..."

Nothing of this is in the current edition of the *Britannica*, where credit for the entry is simply "S.We/Ed."

Lawrence wrote to John Buchan on 20 June 1927:

My father's people were merchants in the Middle Ages: then squires in Leicestershire. In Tudor times they had promoted themselves to soldiering, and had married with a Devon family: by favour of one of these cousins (Sir Walter Raleigh) they got a huge grant of County Meath in Ireland, from Queen Elizabeth: and they lived till the Irish Land Acts did away with much of the estate.

Lawrence here seems to have got his facts wrong, or at least mixed, certainly as regards in what county the original grant of lands was supposedly made. It would be of interest to know his source regarding "merchants in the Middle Ages". What Devon family did the Chapman's marry into? Also, why the lack of reticence now as to what he had earlier allowed D. G. Hogarth to publish? - a point which was raised by Richard Aldington in his 1955 'Biographical Enquiry'.

In a letter dated 28 June 1927, to Robert Graves, his first official biographer, Lawrence wrote:

I) Family. My father's family were Co. Meath in Ireland. A Leicester squire-root, which got a huge grant from Q. Elizabeth, by favour of W. Raleigh, their cousin. Lived thenceforward in Ireland, always particular to marry non-Irish women. My father took name of Lawrence (not even my mother's name) when he left Ireland.

Then Basil Liddell Hart was to write in his Diary, when compiling information for the second official Lawrence biography (1934):

Father's family came from Leicestershire, cousins of Walter Raleigh, at that time. Settled in County Meath, estates round castle....Never intermarried with Irish, always with English or Scot, especially with Yorkshire.

When later commenting upon a draft typescript of Liddell Hart's book, Lawrence wrote:

Your p. 1.
The second paragraph. There are (as I hinted at Hindhead) things not quite desirable in this. Without wanting to censor I suggest alternatives - written with the allusiveness that hints at knowledge refusing to betray itself except between the lines.
'He was of mixed race. His father's family were Elizabethan settlers from England, favoured in gaining land in County Meath by Walter Raleigh, a connection. During three hundred years of Irish domicile they never married into Ireland, but chose their wives from intruders such as themselves, from England, from Holland even. His mother was Island Scotch in feeling and education, but her parentage was part English, part Scandinavian. The sympathy of his home was Irish, all the stronger for being exiled. Wales of the Atlantic coast had no share in him, after his first year.'

Lawrence again repeats the error of in which county the original 16th century grants were made, though there may perhaps be a suspicion that he could have had probable verbal (if nothing else) access to some sources of information not elsewhere disclosed.

Ronald Storrs was responsible for the entry on Lawrence in the *Dictionary of National Biography, 1931-1940 Supplement*, published 1949; but as far as ancestry is concerned only details regarding his mother and father were included.

Twenty years after Lawrence's death, Richard Aldington, in what was to be the first really adverse critique of Lawrence, was to make great play of Lawrence's secrecy about his ancestry and personal genealogy. One can almost hear him say "gullible" as regards the details publicised by Graves and Liddell-Hart, but which had been more or less dictated by Lawrence. Aldington for his part, however, did not appear to have made a serious attempt to check or question any of the bald facts stated in *Burke* about Lawrence's Chapman family ancestry.

It could well have been expected that Jeremy Wilson - in his massive 1989 authorised biography - would have gone into Lawrence's ancestry in some depth. But he too, (and as he supposes so did Lawrence), appeared to have accepted the published details from the acknowledged experts in the field - in this instance the 1918 edition of *Debrett's Illustrated Baronetage*. These do not appear to differ either from those of *Burke*. In his 1988 National Potrait Gallery Exhibition publication *T. E. Lawrence: Lawrence of Arabia*, Wilson reiterates without elaboration the Chapman family's Hinckley origins.

There were thus several separate but connected aspects that had to be researched to determine as far as possible the various truths about this perceived Chapman-Ralegh-Lawrence connection, etc.:

1. That a Chapman family, possibly from the Hinckley area of Leicestershire were related to the famous 16/17th century Devonian - Sir Walter Ralegh;
2. That the brothers John and William Chapman from this family obtained lands in Munster;
3. That this was through their connection with their alleged kinsman;
4. What and where these lands were in Munster;
5. That these same lands were sold subsequently to the 1st Earl of Cork, and the circumstances of such;
6. That there is a provable, or at least reasonably acceptable, unbroken genealogical line from these first Chapman settlers in Ireland down to T. E. Lawrence;
7. How the subsequent Chapman family fared generally over the centuries, down to the time of T. E. Lawrence,

including acquisition of further land and property, and any later disposal.

Beginning with consideration of the Ralegh aspect, one of the first tasks was to enquire of Debrett's Peerage Ltd, and Burke's Peerage, as to whence came their information. Debrett's merely forwarded a list of biographical sources for the names of Chapman and Ralegh; adding that they had hoped that the relationship might have been through Ralegh's mother, Katherine Champernowne, but that that seemed unlikely. Burke's, on the other hand, could only offer to search their original source for a fee of £100 - which offer was not taken up. (From what has now been discovered from subsequent researches Burke's could possibly now be charged £100 to amend their Chapman and other families' entries.)

When it was queried with a correspondent as from whence this authoritatively accepted information might have been derived, the following is the gist of responses to a similar query re. *Burke's Landed Gentry* on the Society of Genealogist's Internet *Mailing List*. Rather than carry out research, Burke was said to have simply sent out forms to members of the families concerned, inviting them to fill out the details of all additions and subtractions since the previous version. (From whence had come the original version?) Burke then took the feedback, and after processing subsequently sent out galley proofs to the correspondents to make any final corrections before printing. The only 'research' records would thus be the respective families' completed forms, the contents of which Burke allegedly accept uncritically. Another correspondent had also queried the accuracy of *Burke*'s, e.g. "sons" should sometimes be "grandsons".

Also to be checked for a Chapman link, of course, were biographies of Ralegh, his many other co-joined families, and his contemporaries - but this was to be without any success. Not knowing the original John and William's father's and mother's Christian names was an obvious stumbling block. This latter point was to soon prove all the more important.

This may be an appropriate point to look briefly at the Ralegh family genealogy. A thesis found useful for this aspect of the research study was that by Michael J. G. Sandford, of 1955: *A History of the Ralegh Family in the Early Tudor Period.* Sandford was to come across a difficulty with the loss of many Ralegh papers during WW2, through enemy bombing at Plymouth and Exeter.

WALTER RALEGH (c.1440-1485) of Fardel in Devon, (whose father William was related by marriage to the Devon families of Courtenay and Pomeroy) married c.1475
KATHERINE CHAMPERNOWNE, daughter of William Champernowne. They had it is believed three sons,
WYMUND, Adam, and Christian.

WYMUND RALEGH (c.1475-1512) of Fardel, married c.1500
ELIZABETH, daughter of Sir Richard EDGCUMBE of Cotehele, Cornwall, who was Comptroller of the King's Household, and Walter Ralegh's ward whilst in his minority following his father's death. They had a son
WALTER, and daughter Joan.

WALTER RALEGH (c.1505-1581) of Hayes Barton, East Budleigh, Devon. In the 1581 Inquisition *post mortem* his name was variously spelt: Rawleye, Rawleygh, Rawley, Rawligh, Rawlighe, and Rawle. He married:

1stly c.1526 JOAN, daughter of Sir John DRAKE of Exmouth, Devon. She was 2nd cousin of Sir Francis Drake, and had a brother John who married a sister of Sir Richard Grenville (of the *Revenge* fame). Joan Ralegh died June 1530. They had two sons
George (who married into the Gilbert family), and John.

2ndly in 1531 a Mrs DARRELL, widow, of London, about whom almost nothing is known. They had one daughter
Mary.

3rdly c.1548 KATHERINE GILBERT (widow of Otho Gilbert), and daughter of Sir PHILIP CHAMPERNOWNE of Modbury, Devon. Her mother, Katherine, daughter of Sir Edward Carew, of Devon, was very highly connected, and among the gentlewomen appointed in 1536 to attend the infant princess Elizabeth, and possibly held her at her christening. "A woman of noble wit and of good and godly opinion", and able to read. Elizabeth was to say: "She brynketh me up from the cradell to the throne." Katherine's sister, Joan, married Sir Anthony Denny. Walter and Katherine had two sons,

Carew c.1550 (later Sir), and the more famous WALTER c.1552 (later Sir), and a daughter Margaret.

The early Ralegh crest (dated 1537) was carved on the end of the family pew in All Saints church, East Budleigh. Walter and his two sons from his first marriage were accused of being privateers. Also, he and kinsman Sir Arthur Champernowne were accused in 1548 of collecting a number of armed persons and committing personal assaults. His third wife's sons were to outshine those by his first wife, and she was probably responsible for all five of her sons possibly being at Court together.

WALTER (c.1552-1618) of East Budleigh, Devon, and London, and later Sherborne in Dorset, married c.1592

ELIZABETH THROCKMORTON, a daughter of Sir Nicholas and Anne (née Carew) Throckmorton. Walter and Elizabeth married clandestinely whilst he was a favourite at Court, being Captain of the Queen's Guard and she was a maid-of-honour to Queen Elizabeth. The latter showed her displeasure by imprisoning both in the Tower of London for a while.

During his lifetime he signed himself RALEGH, but there were some 70 other contemporary spellings, both English and foreign, based on the phonetic 'raw-lee' - a point to be borne in mind.

No Chapman has been found to be connected to any of these marriages.

Many of Ralegh's relatives will continue to be mentioned in these pages, in order to draw up a clearer picture of their inter-relationship, and involvement in the Irish situation. This in turn may enable one to see a pattern which can help determine those seven points mentioned on page 10 above.

The use of the expression 'cousin-german' in *Burke* etc. is somewhat ambiguous. It can mean either 'first cousin', i.e. a child of one's uncle or aunt; or figuratively a person closely related, or even just a near relative. In the Dorset County Museum at Dorchester there is an early copy of *Burke's Peerage and Baronetage*, dated 1828. In the Chapman entry of this edition is included a small but important detail omitted from later editions. It is there mentioned that Ralegh was a 'maternal' cousin german. This in itself did not really carry the search any more forward, but if accepted as truth it somewhat narrowed down further avenues of genealogical research. It also made it even more imperative to check and double-check all items of information that may be gathered. One wonders why this relevant word 'maternal' was subsequently omitted.

Appropriate published 16th/17th century *Heralds' Visitations* have been examined, as being almost primary evidence even nearer to being contemporaneous - though not necessarily reliably accurate. The Pedigrees in these *Visitations* may not have been any more reliable than *Burke* or *Debrett*, being dependent on what Heralds were told by the titled. There is a paucity of genealogical dates in the Pedigrees; and probably the only queries raised at the time would have been over any discrepancies regarding coats of arms. Thus unsurprisingly they proved fruitless.

The Mormon *International Genealogical Index* (the *IGI*) not unexpectedly was also non-informative. Using this *IGI* as a research tool relies on it being a full, complete and accurate transcription and compilation of church records relating to births, baptisms and marriages, though unfortunately neither deaths nor burials are included. But for obvious reasons the accuracy of such early records as there were is certainly less than perfect. Births and marriages for various reasons may have been 'hidden' or not recorded, recorded incorrectly, or proper records subsequently become destroyed, damaged or indecipherable through rodents, insects, damp, fire, or even just lost. There has been human vandalism in that some registers were wantonly used to light fires, or as wrapping papers. On the other hand, the sheer amount of information remaining is such that not all of it has yet been put into the *IGI*. Parish Registers of such events did not start in any case until 1538. Any *IGI* records before that date are thus derived from other sources, including submissions from families and other researchers - whose information must of necessity be somewhat suspect or biased.

Genealogy cannot, alas, be an exact science, and is even less so now with the advent of medical technology and artificial insemination. 'It is a wise man who knows his father', as the saying goes.

Still to be proved was the initial Leicestershire origins, and of course the Ralegh connection. The Leicestershire Public Record Office had been asked to provide photocopies of extant Chapman wills of the mid to late 1500s, but again no such link was found in those listed or provided.

Eventually there was reason to contact Mr Steve Chapman in Dorset. He generously supplied copious details of similar investigations, dating from the mid-1800s, by members of another branch of the Chapman family from Leicestershire. They too were unsuccessfully still trying to find this elusive Chapman-Ralegh family connection. Included in the correspondence was a *Pedigree of the Family of Chapman of Whitwick, Ashby-De-La-Zouch, Upton, Etc., Co. Leicester*, compiled by J. Paul Rylands FSA, in 1908, reprinted from *Miscellanea Genealogica Et Heraldica*. This Pedigree unfortunately only started from the 1680s. In Rylands preamble to the *Pedigree* he said that much of the information came from Miss Jane Chapman (1779-1870) about 1868. (Had she been one of the original family informers to *Burke's Peerage and Baronetage* before 1828?) He further said that it was a family tradition (traceable to the early 18th century) that this branch of the Chapman family originated from Hinckley, and were of the same stock as the 16th century William Chapman of Ireland, who moved there under the auspices of his cousin Sir Walter Ralegh, and founded the family of Chapman of Killua Castle, co. Westmeath. This did not of course really advance the search.

PEDIGREE of Dame SARAH, Widow of Sir JOHN CHAPMAN; and of GRACE, Wife of JOSIAH ROBARTS. [Appendix to HINCKLEY, to face p. 360*.]

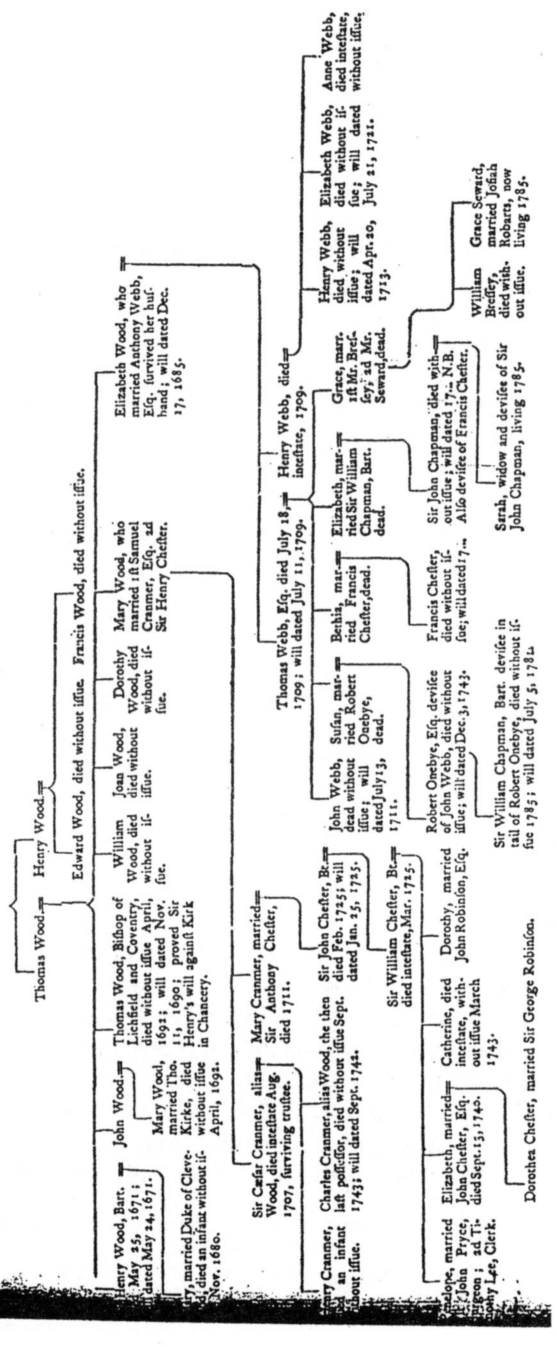

Meanwhile in the *Index To Printed Pedigrees Contained In County & Local Histories, Etc.* by Charles Bridger, there was listed *The History and Antiquities of Hinckley, etc.* of 1790. This *History* was said to contain a Chapman Pedigree. When examined it was found that this Pedigree did in fact contain some Chapman content - see illustration opposite.

On checking with Cokayne's *The Complete Baronetcy* it appears that this baronetcy was created on 27 June 1720, with Sir William Chapman of London the 1st baronet. He had been born c.1670, knighted in 1714, and died 7 May 1737. The baronetcy then passed to his son John of Hertfordshire, born c.1710, M.P. for Taunton 1741-1747, who on his death on 29 January 1781 left no surviving children. The baronetcy thus passed to John's brother, William of Suffolk, born 1714, and who died on 9 February 1785 in London, again without surviving children. Therefore this baronetcy became extinct. It should be remembered that the Chapman baronetcy of Lawrence's father was not created until 1782. Is this then where the tradition of Hinckley origins had perhaps mistakenly arisen? Thus unfortunately this particular Hinckley material was not to prove helpful.

Clifford Chapman of Florida was later to draw attention to *IGI* records of a Rychard Chapman of Leicester, born c.1538, who was the father (in order) of a John, William, Thomas, and Richard, born between 1563-1577. Checking with the imperfect Mormon *IGI*, the baptism of William was found on 6 October 1566 at Lutterworth. Though this may have been seen as promising at first sight, whilst still at the beginning of researches, these particular Chapmans had really been born too late for this study; and in the light of what was already being discovered could practically be discounted.

WERE THEY REALLY CALLED CHAPMAN?

Rylands, in his 1908 *Pedigree*, had referred to Nichols' *History and Antiquities of Leicestershire*, but he was naturally only looking for Chapmans. However, in Volume II, Part I of Nichols' *History* an interesting Pedigree was found, headed 'STEMMATA Familiarum de ROHAUD, GOLDINGTON, CHAMPERNOON, BOZON, & DEENE.' The relevant part of the Pedigree is reproduced opposite. Of particular interest are the Champernoon entries.

It will be seen that the first appearance of a Champernoon is Sir Thomas in 1360/1, but his place of abode is unfortunately not given. Neither is it of his son Richard, nor grandson also named Richard. However, Sir Thomas's great-grandson Hugh de Champernoon of 1442/3 is shown as of Modbury, co. Devon. This is the very place whence the Champernowne family line had originated, and into which family the Raleghs had twice married. Hugh's son John, at the time of his death in 1475/6, is shown in possession of the Leicestershire properties

of the manors of Worthington and Kimcote, and part of the manor of Clauston.

Seemingly only having two daughters, this particular Champernowne line ends. But the Modbury connection continues through the line of John's brother, William, down to Hugh's grandson Sir John c.1500.

It was further stated by Nichols that

Maud [i.e. Matilda], the youngest daughter of Peter de Goldrington was married to Sir Alan Rohaud, knight; whose heir-general was in the reign of Edward III [1327-1377] married to [Thomas de] Champernoon, of Modbury, co. Devon, from whom descended Sir John Champernon, knight, who died seised of part of Clawston 1476 [Esch. 15 Edw. IV. n. 30], whose daughter and coheir, Blanch, brought it in marriage to Robert lord Willoughby of Broke.

We thus have our first extended family link between Ralegh and Leicestershire - wherein lies Hinckley.

STEMMATA Familiarum de ROHAUD, GOLDINGTON[5], CHAMPERNOON[6], BOZON[7], & DEENE[8].
(From MS. CHETWYND.)

Rohaud, lord of the manor of Eaſton, co. Oxford.

Peter de Goldington, lord of Worthington manor, ob. 37 Hen. III.

Alan Rohaud, knt. 7 E. I. 33 E. I. = Matilda, dau. and coheir, brought her huſband the manor of Worthington.

Dioniſia. = Milo de Haſtinges. ob. ſ. p.

Iſabella, widow of ſir Rob. Bardolſe, and heir to her ſiſter Dioniſia. = Ralph Bozon, of Claxton, 34 Edw. I.

Henry Rohaud, knt. of Clauſton, = Roſe, daughter of ſir John de Bigbury, knt.

John Bozon, 34 E. I.

Roger Rohaud, 20 E. III. = Eleanor, dau. of Rich. Lovell, knt. 20 E. III.

William Bozon[9], temp. E. II. E. III.

Elizabeth, dau. and heir. = Thomas de Champernoon, knt. 34 E. III.

John Bozon.

Ric. de Champernoon, knt. ob. 1418. = Catharine, dau. of Ralph Daubigny.

John Bozon.

Nich. de Deene, or Deane. = Catharine, dau. and heir of Robert Pedwardine, brought him the manors of Pedwardine and Clipſton, co. Northampton.

Ric. de Champernoon, 2 Hen. V. = Elizabeth, dau. of John lord Bonvile.

Henry Bozon, knt. = Catharine, dau. of Rob. Markham, of Cotham, co. Nott.

John Deene, of Barroughby, co. Linc. in right of his wife, dau. of ſir John Paynel, of Barrowby and Boothby, co. Linc. 18 C.

Hugh de Champernoon, of Modbury, co. Devon, ob. 20 H. VI. = Alice, dau. and heir of John Bois.

John Champernoon, knt. ob. ſeiſed of the manors of Worthinton and Kimcote, and part of the manor of Clauſton, 15 E. IV.

Will. Champernoon. = Thomaſine, dau and heir of Tho. Chitterley, of Chitterley.

1. Richard Bozon of Clauſton, knt. the laſt male heir[10]. = Dorothy[11], alias Mary, dau and heir, ob 26 H. VIII. = Will. Vernon, 2d huſband.

John Champernoon, of Modbury, knt. = Mary, dau. of Philip Courtney, of Molland.

Joan, wife of Henry Savile, of Lupſett, co. Ebor.

Blanch, mar. to Rob. lord Willoughby of Broke. [See the deſcent from this Blanch in Kimcote.]

Joan, mar. to .... Talbot, ob. ſ. p. 24 Hen. VII.

5. Agnes[12], dau. and coh. mar. 1ſt. Hen. Babington; and, 2. Francis Moore, of Frickley, co. Ebor.

2. Mary, mar. Joh. Worſley[13], of Helpſton, co. Northamp.

3. Margaret, mar. Rich. Clopton, of Melford.

4. Alice, mar. Tho. Lewis, of Saperton.

1. Elizabeth, mar. R. Paynel, of Boothby, and had the manor of Worthington.

The Champernoon arms are given as:

Gules, billetté, Or, a saltire vaire, and a crescent for difference.

Burke's General Armory states that the crest for the above is 'A swan sitting proper holding in the beak a gold horseshoe.' Crests for some other Champernowne arms are given as: 'A lion's head erased argent semée of pellets and ducally crowned or', and 'A demi-lion argent holding a cross formée fitchée or.'

The above Champernoon arms incorporate a couple of heraldic charges from other Champernowne family branches quoted in Baring-Gould and Twigge's *Armory*, with its inconsistent spellings:

Champnowne: *Gules crucili formy formed fitch or, a saltire varry.*
Champnon of Devon: *Gules, saltier verry 12 billets or.*
Chambernon of Devon: *Gules, a saltier verry 12 (cross-crosslets) or.*
Champnon of Devon: *Gules, a saltier verry.*
Champernowne of Devon: *Gules, a saltire vair between 12 crosses formée fitchée or.*
Champernowne: *Gules, semée of 24 billets or, a saltire vair.*
Champernowne of Devon: *Gules, a saltire vair between 12 billets or.*
Champernoun of Devon: *Gules, sawter varry argent, et b. semy (cross-crosslets) or.*
Champernoun of Devon: *Gules, a sawter varry argent, et b. 12 (billets) or.*
Champernon of Devon: *Gules, a sawter varry argent, et b.*
Champnowne of Modbury: *Gules, billytie (cruxillie fytch) or. a salter verry.*
Champnowne of Exeter: *Gules, a salter verry between 3 bessants.*
Champnowne of Bere Ferrers: *Gules, a salter verry between 3 crusills flurt fitche or.*
Champnowne of Bere Ferrers: *Argent, a lyon rampant gules, a bordure ingreyled sable.*

It is noted in the *Heralds' Visitation of the County of Devon* that the arms of Rohant and Coldington are associated with those of the Champernowne family. But whereas Nichols shows that William, who married Thomasine, daughter of Thomas Chitterley, was the son of Hugh de Champernoon, the *Visitation* gives Oliver Champernon as his father.

Now is the time to more closely see just who the Champernownes were, their ancestry, etc. When comparing 'official' Pedigrees with that compiled in 1953 by C. E. Champernowne, further details are found, as well as several differences.

According to Loyd in *The Origins of some Anglo-Norman Families* this family's original home was quite possibly at Cambernon, in Manche, Normandy, France. In 1166 there are Henry de Camperburne, and Jordan de Capernun whose mother Mabira was a daughter of Robert earl of Gloucester and sister of earl William. In 1172 Jordan de Campo Arnulfi owed the service of one knight in Normandy, having himself the service of two knights. Campus Arnulfi is some twelve miles morth of Cerences. Between 1189 and 1199 Richard de Cambernof gave to the canons regular of Yvrandes the church of St-Cornier, a gift confirmed by his brother Jordan de Champernon. In a charter c.1170, Mabira confirmed to this priory the gift of her son Jordan de Campo Ernulfi of the church of Maisoncelles.

The above Henry is thought to be the same Henry Champernowne who c.1159 is found at Clist in Devon, and who married Rohesia de Tracy of the same place.

In this direct line at Modbury was the same Thomas, son of Sir Richard Champernoon, born c.1314, who married Eleanor, daughter and sole heiress of Sir Roger Rohart of Kincote, Leicester - though the Rohaud Pedigree gives it as Elizabeth. As we already know, she brought her husband the manors of Clauston/Claxton and Worthington in Leicestershire.

At Devon Record Office, (reference 3940M/N2, Beer/Bere Ferrers), is some 1908 correspondence with the vicar. In the *Calendar Inquisitions post mortem* the will of Alexander Champernown was proved in 1443. Roger

Champernowne was said to be his eldest son in the *Calendar*, page 333, 5 Edward IV 1465-66. A Roger Champernowne had died on 3 May 1401 according to Bishop Stafford's *Register*, having been Chaplain of the Hospital of St Gabriel at Clyst.

The Leicestershire manors later went to John Champernoon /Champernowne, born c.1412, and who married c.1435 Elizabeth, daughter and co-heiress of William Bigbury of Bigbury (3 miles south of Modbury). He died 3 April 1475. In the *Inquisition post mortem* of 1476 there is given the following properties in

Leycester; Kilmandcote manor, Lydington/Lydynton manor, Worthrynton, Caxton manor, Bevere Castr' Membr'

as well as Devon properties.

In the *Calendar*, page 370, 15 Edward IV, 1476, a Johannes Champernowne left

enormous properties in Warwickshire, Leycestershire, North'tonshire, Linconshire, Devon and Cornwall.

This Pedigree line continued at Modbury, with a branch eventually settling in 1559 at Dartington, also in Devon.

What can be learned from studies of the Champernowne associated localities in Devon? See sketch map opposite.

BERE FERRERS

As described by Arthur Mee, it is

Attractively set on the Tavy estuary, it looks across the water to lovely woods.

It is a parish in the hundred of Roborough, south Devon, approached by a winding road which drops down to the old part of the village, which is on a bit of an isolated peninsula bounded on the west by the navigable river Tamar, and on the east by the Tavey. The village takes part of its name from the De Ferrers family of Normandy,

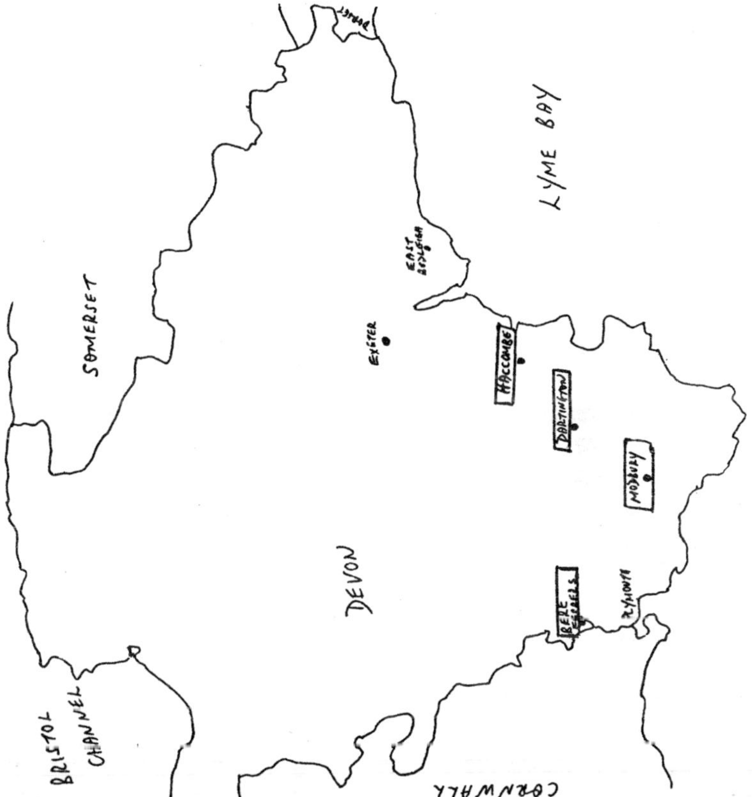
LYME BAY
SOMERSET
EXETER
HACCOMBE
DARTINGTON
MODBURY
DEVON
BRISTOL CHANNEL
CORNWALL

who lived here since Norman times. There was a castellated and fortified mansion and park of the Champernownes at Bere Ferrers, but it is difficult to say now where it stood. Possibly the Barton near the church is part of the building, where other relics of antiquity are found, and the old barn and a remaining wall near the house show signs of having been fortified. John Champernowne c.1412-1475 married c.1435 Elizabeth Bigbury of Bigbury (three miles south of Modbury).

The 14th century church of St. Andrew is near the river. The living is a rectory valued in the king's book at £24.1s.0½d; net income £700; patron Viscount Valletort. Alexander Champernowne (c.1370-c.1420) of Modbury, married Joan, the eldest of the three daughters of (Sir) Martin, the last of the Ferrers, who brought Bere Ferrers as her dower. Alexander is shown as Patron of the living in 1417.

His son Sir Roger Champernowne (c.1400-c.1455) is shown as lord of the manor of Bere Alston and an M.P. for Devon in 1433 and 1436; and Patron of Bere Ferrers in 1452. He has a fine large memorial fixed on the west wall in the church's north transept. This memorial was apparently originally before the altar step in the transept. It has a cross with degrees incised upon it, and the sacred heart with an IHS monogram in the centre. There is an inscription:

Hic jacet Roger Champnoun Armiger cui aie ppicietur de ame

a shortened form of:

Hic jacet Roger Champnoun Armiger cuius anime propricietur deus amen ("Here lies Roger Champnoun armour-bearer [or armiger] for whose soul prayers may be offered to God")

Another son of Alexander and Joan Champernowne, the John who died 1475, left a daughter Blanch who married Sir Robert Willoughby de Broke - see the Rohaud Pedigree earlier in this chapter.

According to the *Church Guide* and *Parish History* there was also a record of a stone under the main altar inscribed "Orate pro Willma Champernoun" - "Pray for William Champernoun". William Champernoun had married Matilda Joan, daughter of Sir William Ferrers (c.1280-c.1337), and although he lived at Tywardreath in Cornwall, when he died in 1304 it seems he was respected enough by the Ferrers family to be buried this far from his home.

MODBURY

The parish of Modbury is about six miles from east to west, and three from north to south. It is in general very fertile, except a little in the eastern part. It is for the most part bare of timber.

The town of Modbury lies about a mile to the westward of the central part of the parish, and contains about 200 houses. It consists principally of four streets, which meet at right angles in the market-place. It is a medieval market town, developed from a Saxon settlement. In 1328 an annual Fair began, on St. George's Day, after which the church is dedicated. In 1362 Thomas de Campo Arnulphi became lord of Modbury.

The 16th century timbered *Exeter Inn* is the pride of Broad Street, striking in its black and white. As Arthur Mee wrote about Modbury in 1938:

It has lost much, including its ancient priory and much of its great house, but it has still its 13th century church, with the tombs of its crusaders...Under a recess Sir John Champernowne lies in 15th century armour, with his feet on a lion; he used to play bowls in the churchyard when it was the bowling green of the great house next door. Only one wing remains of it, the rest having been burned down by the Parliament men in 1642. But the Champernownes were Royalists in spite of rebuffs and not for favours received, for they were harshly treated.

At the top of Church Street, on the west side near the church entrance, the great family of Champernowne lived at the Court House from the 14th to the end of the 17th century, being fortified by Richard Champernowne in 1334. It was severely damaged during two Civil War skirmishes and was later demolished, and the stone dispersed and sold for building material elsewhere. Scant traces of the Court House, and perhaps the medieval Priory too, remain in walls near Modbury church, and pieces of old heavy granite moulded stones in the lower, western area of the town are incorporated into newer buildings.

Modbury, a place for multiplicity of ancient houses and fertility of soil, inferior to few in this county...Sir James Okeston, that died without issue, who by commandment of King Edward the 2d [reigned 1307-1327], conveyed Modbury and all his lands (formerly granted) unto Sir Richard Champernowne, knight, descended from Joan, [widow of Ralph Vaultort, and who later married Sir Alexander Okeston, knight], whom Edmund Earl of Cornwal calleth by the name of sister, in a grant made by him to the said Richard and Joan of the assize of bread and ale in Ann, 12, Edward the 1st. This name of Champernon hath been very numerous, and have planted themselves at divers places, as Bear, Umberley, Insworke, Ilfracombe, Dartington, Bigbery, Tawton, this place, &c. who in ancient evidences are written *de Campo Arnulphi*. The inheritor of these lands married the daughter of Sir Anthony Cope in Oxfordshire, knight, his father Sir Arthur, a worthy commander in the wars, the daughter and heir of Crewkern, his grandsire, the daughter and heir of Sir Richard Edgcombe, knight.

Modbury is a strange solitary town in a dell, between green hills, without trees and without water.

Much of the land belongs to Eton College. The 13th century church of St. George, which stands on a height, is a large handsome, though plain building: the lofty spire in particular, (which was probably new-built about 1621 after being struck by lightning, and might be considered more of a repair) is considered as a master-piece of good work. There had been major reconstruction between 1400-1500. The church suffered during the Civil War, including loss of it's Rood Screen. It is also remarkable for a very fine marble font, and three large and commodious galleries, erected in 1716.

It is rather bare of monumental decorations;...From several niches, however, and mutilated remains of statues (especially one of the Champernownes family, in compleat armour [William died 1464]) which appears to have lain there in state, it is evident that the church was once more pompously ornamented than it is at present [1806].

The *Church Guide* further mentions the well-carved figure of Sir John Champernowne, 1457-1503, lying in his canopied recess, but nothing about the lion upon which his missing feet lie according to Mee. Sir John's Yorkist sympathies are supposedly shown by the white roses carved in his collar and sword belt. He was knighted at the marriage of Prince Arthur to Catherine of Aragon, and although spending much of his time at his Oxfordshire manor of Aston Rowant he wished to be buried at Modbury which had been the family seat since 1323. Tradition has it that his feet were broken off when Cromwell's soldiers stabled their horses in the church.

There is a much later slate memorial to other Champernownes:

OBLIVIO
Here Lieth the Body of Philip
Champernoun Esq: Obit 26 July 1684
And Margaret Champernoun his
Daughter. Obit 26 March.
In the year) of her age 30
) of our Lord 1715
OBLIVIO

The coat of arms on this memorial is based on that devised by Sir Richard Champernowne c.1606 re. a claim against the Blount family estate. The crest in these arms is an ostrich holding a horseshoe. The motto is *Duriora Virtus* - 'Strength through Endurance'. The memorial had once been set on the church floor and became badly eroded, but twenty quarterings can still be made out. The Modbury estate was inherited in 1323, with later marriages adding further properties, so that by the early 1400s there was also property in London. Richard Champernowne fortified the mansion house in 1334. The south chancel chapel and the south transept together form the Modbury House aisle. A John Edward Champernown was vicar of Modbury 1910-1921.

It is also noted that on the church's interior WW1/WW2 war memorial, under 1914-1918 there is a J.E.CHAMPERNOWNE.

In March 1543 Henry VIII raised musters, to be ready at an hour's warning, by sending letters to the gentry of the counties, including Sir Philip Champernowne of Modbury. During the Tudor period the Champernownes of Modbury had a band of musicians. Tales about it were noted in the *Report and Transactions of the Devonshire Association, Vol. LXXVII* 1946. Henry VIII got Sir Philip Champernowne (c.1502-45) to Windsor with his band, and kept him there, presumably without payment, so that Sir Philip had to sell some manors. A grandson of Sir Philip, possibly Henry, later declined a similar honour, and had to forfeit 19 manors to Elizabeth. Another version of the earlier incident may be found at the foot of page 272 of Burke's *Commoners, Vol. II.*

Though according to Arthur Mee:

The 16th century Sir Richard [should it not be Sir Philip?] kept here a company of musicians whose fame reached Henry the Eighth, so that he summoned them to Court, Sir Richard [sic] took them to Windsor in costly new liveries, but they remained at the court unnoticed and were finally dismissed unheard, Sir Richard [sic] being left to pay all charges, When Elizabeth heard of him and summoned him to Court, the bold Sir Richard [sic] answered that his last visit had crippled him, whereupon the queen declared that she would cripple him farther and took away his manors...The family fortunes survived these shocks, but the burning of the house in the Civil War was the last blow it could stand for its loyalty to the Tudors and Stuarts,

With the family having to dispose of so much property under either Henry VIII or Elizabeth, it would have been perhaps an incentive for some members to try their luck in Ireland during the several plantations. There are, however, still quite a number of Champernowne entries in the Modbury parish registers between 1622 and 1717.

The 1908 correspondent with the vicar of Modbury was to write:

> The alabaster Champernowne effigy at Modbury is not so mutilated or disfigured with peoples' names as the one at Collington, and I hope to get plate glass in front, but I have no hope of any assistance from the Champernowne family in either Bere Ferrers or Modbury restoration.

Enclosed with one letter was a bookplate for Richard Champernowne: 'Ostrich with horseshoe, and X with twelve billets. Motto: *Duriora Virtus.*'

The memorial was replaced in the church after 1870 renovations. It was probably dated 1465, being the death of Roger Champernowne, the eldest son of Alexander (son of Sir Richard Champernowne of Modbury) and his wife Joan, daughter and co-heiress of Martin Ferrers, lord of Bere Ferrers. Alexander Champernowne lent money to Henry V to regain French possessions, dying in 1443, with his son Roger succeeding to the castle and manor of Bere Ferrers. He died in 1465, without issue, being succeeded by his brother Sir John, who had one daughter Blanche, and heiress to the large Beer Ferrers and Modbury properties of her father, including many manors in distant counties. Blanche married Sir Robert Willoughby, youngest son of Sir John Willoughby of Lincolnshire; and brought all these estates to her husband. Sir Robert became the first Baron Willoughby de Broke in 1491, dying in 1502, and being buried at Collington, where there is an alabaster altar tomb to his memory.

Wimpston is a considerable farm, and also a manor. At one time it belonged to the Champernowne family - possibly being one of those that had to be disposed of in the reigns of Henry VIII and Elizabeth I.

DARTINGTON

It is a place to be visited, about a mile from Shinner's Bridge. Turn off the A384 at Dartington church, (an 1880 replica of the old parish church of St. Mary that originally stood close to the Hall), then drive down a narrow winding road until the estate grounds and Arts Centre complex is reached. It is superbly situated in the centre of some 850 acres of rich land, wood, water, and lawn, on an undulating green rise above a sweeping bend of the river. Park in the sign-posted car park.

The Hall itself is approached across a forecourt flanked by trees. As the entry is made to the main north courtyard by a small door in the great portals of the entrance block, the full beauty of the buildings is seen. The baronial mansion is very ancient, among terraced gardens above the River Dart, and from the walls and foundations appear to have consisted of a double quadrangle, divided by a spacious hall, and which, with the state apartments in the western quadrangle, is supposed to have been built by Holland, Duke of Exeter.

The courtyard is under the arch, and opposite (on the west) is the Great Hall, a roofless ruin in 1925, but now beautifully restored with timbers drawn from the estate. The Great Hall with its line of seven 16 feet wide windows, has magnificant hammer-beam roof timbers, and the long massive fireplace. Beyond it is the main residential block. On the east the huge reconstructed medieval kitchens, now the dining hall.

Immediately to the right is a huge, graceful swamp cypress tree, nurtured by a hidden wellspring beneath its roots. To the east and west are continuous ranges of medieval buildings, originally living accommodation for the high-ranking staff members. Those on the west have arched, open entrance porches.

Ahead is the glorious complex of medieval entrance porch with its clock tower and silvery bells. On the centre ceiling boss inside the porch is carved the personal badge of Richard II, a white hart, surrounded by the wheat ears of his half-brother and adviser John Holand, later Earl of Huntingdon and Duke of Exeter, to whom he gave Dartington.

Behind the hall in the gardens is the restored tilting yard, with terraced grassy banks and twelve enormous clipped yews looking like giant skittles. Modern tournaments, outdoor plays, masques and *son et lumière* presentations are sometimes held here.

The living is a rectory, valued in the king's books at £36. 4s. 4½d, and in the patronage of the Champernowne family. The church of St. Mary was in the later English style, with a chancel and tower of more ancient date; the pulpit was richly carved, and in the chancel was a monument to one of the Champernownes, whose mother was preceptress to Queen Elizabeth. Only the tower of the original church alongside the Hall now stands, containing some Champernowne memorials. The parish registers for baptisms start in 1542, marriages in 1538, and burials in 1539. The early registers have been damaged, with the beginning and end entries illegible.

On the wall of the old church tower is a plaster memorial, dated 1578, to Sir Arthur Champernowne (c.1520-1578), his wife Mary, and their eight surviving children. In Rev. Polwhele's *History of Devon*, it is described as

> representing ten figures, six men completely clad in armour, two women, and two children, seven kneeling and three standing; ornamented with several coats of arms but no inscription.

To give some indication of the sex and seniority of these children, the monument seemingly shows the figures from left to right:

> teenage Girl, young Girl, teenage Boy, two young Men with beards, young Child, older teenage Boy, young Man with beard, Father, Mother.

Close by is a yew tree which was 100 years old when Sir Arthur knew it.

The estate was bought from the Hollands by Sir Arthur Champernowne in 1559. He built a new residential wing on the west side of the Great Hall, still known as the Private House, now the Elmhirst Centre. According to Mee, it was during

> its Tudor period when the owner was advised by Raleigh [sic] about planning the gardens...

The Champernownes ran the 2,000 acre estate until 1921, making further alterations and enlargements before they began a long losing battle against the decline of their fortunes. There was first the sale of art treasures and land, and then finally the remaining estate itself in 1921.

Leland, in his *Itinerary in England & Wales, Volume I*, began c.1538, was to comment:

Dartington Park half a mile above Totenes Bridge on the same ripe [bank of a river or brook] of the water that Totenes is. In this park is a great manor place that longid to the Duke of Excester. S.Liger, that maried the Duches of Excester, kept house in this place.

Then Leland noted in *Volume V*:

Dartyngton, the fayre and goodly lordship by Totnes in Devonshire, was the Lords of Audleys, sens by attayntur the Duke of Excester, namyd Holland, that cawsyd his hole howsholde there to drinke wyne browght out of Fraunce. He was Admirall of England, and Sir Baldwine Fulfirte a Knight of the Sepulchre was his undar admiralle.
Corteney Marquese of Excester had a late this Dartington.

HACCOMBE

This is one of the smallest parishes in England, just a few miles south-west of Teignmouth, in Devon. According to Mee:

The [700 year-old] church was built as the chapel of an earlier house, and its door had been used as if it were the family stable, horseshoes being nailed on it to commemorate the hair-brained escapade in which Carew of Haccombe challenged Champernowne of Dartington to a swimming race on horseback. They rode into Tor Bay and Champernowne's horse swam till it sank, Carew's [horse] bringing back both riders. Only one of the shoes remains, but the nail-holes show that the four were arranged in a quatrefoil.

What of the early John Champernowne's (c.1412-1475) properties in Leicestershire, mentioned in the Rohaud Pedigree, etc., and were they in the Hinckley area? See sketch map overleaf.

HINCKLEY

A market town, being a place then of narrow streets of old timbered houses with their thatched roofs. The Elizabethan commercial area with its muddle of tiled and gabled roofs. The church tower and nave date from c.1300, with rich coloured glass windows; plus a 15th century brass of a lady.

BELVOIR CASTLE

This is probably the "Bevue Castr" mentioned, but it is all of 33 miles N.E. of Hinckley. The 900-year old 'castle' itself, although just within the north-east boundary of Leicestershire, stands high on an isolated spur of the Lincolshire Wolds, home of the Dukes of Rutland. Round about below in the Vale of Belvoir are the current 22 manors of the Dukedom. Around 1500 Belvoir was in the ownership of the Lords Ros, when one of this line married the daughter of a St Leger, presumably from Devon. The Dukes of Rutland are descended from the Lords Ros.

CLAUSTON

Also known at one time as Caseton or 'Caxton manor', but probably in reality Claxton (or Long Clawson) in the hundred of Framland, in the north of Leicestershire, 26 miles N.E. of Hinckley. It is situated in the Vale of Belvoir, being of some 2,800 acres. The living is a discharge vicarage, valued in the king's books at £9.10s.2d; net income £105; patron is Lord Godolphin. The 13th century church is of St. Remigius.

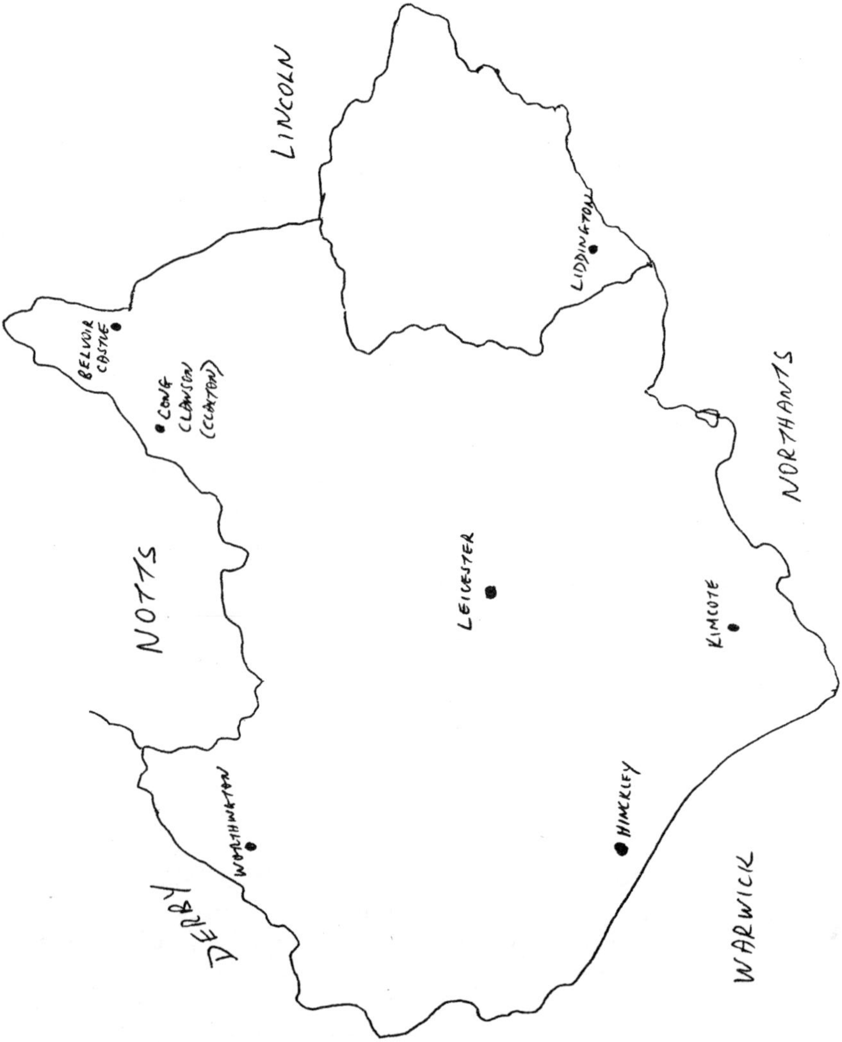
LINCOLN
LIDDINGTON
BELVOIR CASTLE
LONG CLAWSON (CLAXTON)
NORTHANTS
NOTTS
LEICESTER
KIMCOTE
WORTHINGTON
HINCKLEY
DERBY
WARWICK

KIMCOTE

Also known as Kilmondcote or 'Kilmandcote manor', is even closer to Hinckley at 10½ miles eastwards. There is the church of All Saints. The living is a rectory, valued (1844) in the king's books at £20.16s.3d. The patron is Lord Willoughby de Broke - a name found at Bere Ferrers in Devon (*q.v.*).

LIDDINGTON

Or Lyddington/Lydington/Lydnton), is now in Rutland, 27½ miles east of Hinckley. According to Arthur Mee:

Spreading itself through a picturesque valley, it is rich with a fine old [14th century] church and its famous Bede House,

WORTHINGTON

This is only 16 miles north of Hinckley as the crow flies, and comprises nearly 1,500 acres. It is a chapelry in the parish of Breedon, in the hundred of Goscote, Leicestershire. The living is a perpetual curacy, net income £100 (1844).

- - - - -

It has already been shown with the example of Ralegh that spelling of surnames of this period was inconsistent, depending on a listener's understanding of a speaker's pronunciation, especially if it was in a broad west-country dialect such as that of Devon. Similarly, a person's writing was not always consistent or easily readable, especially as Tudor writing was prone to abbreviation. Thus it is not improbable that under certain circumstances the name of Champernowne could gradually degenerate into Chapman. This is a theory that it will be endeavoured to substantiate in this study.

Michael J.G. Sandford's thesis on the Ralegh Family to a certain extent confirmed the Champernowne origins of Chapman. As is known, Sir Walter Ralegh's father's third wife was Katherine Champernowne, but his grandfather had also married a Champernowne. Katherine seems to have had seven siblings, five at least being boys - as shown by the Dartington's old church monument. The younger ones, with little or no prospect of much in the way of an inheritance, would thus have been ideal recruits to have gone out into the world - especially overseas - to seek their fortune, either as mercenaries or settlers.

When this idea became evident the author was reminded of a book previously read at the Dorset County Museum, about the Western Rebellion of 1549. As a punishment certain church bells in Cornwall and Devon were taken away. By a grant of King Edward VI, dated 2 December 1550, the clappers of these bells were given as a loyalty reward to Sir Arthur Champernon and John Chichester. These were subsequently sold on, and in the churchwardens accounts for the parish, this was done in the names of "Sir Arture Chapman & John Chechester". This was the first item of proof, being all the more persuasive considering it was a record from their home county of Devon.

In 1553/1554 there was a further rising in the West Country, in sympathy with the attempted deposing of Mary, a Catholic, in favour of Elizabeth, a Protestant. Sir Gawen Carew was one of the leaders. Kinsman Sir Arthur Champernowne approved, though support fell short of armed revolt, but his arrest was ordered. Sir Arthur was imprisoned in 1554 for his part in the plot against the marriage in the July of Mary to Philip of Spain.

From March 1558 until April 1559 Sir Arthur assisted in the defence of the Devon coast against a feared French invasion. At one time he was a guarantor of Walter Ralegh for £2,000. He bought some of the Ralegh property in 1563, having grown in prosperity in the early years of Elizabeth's reign.

But where do the original John and William Champernowne, alias Chapman, of county Kerry in Ireland, fit in to all this? Sir Arthur Champernowne had eight children on his 1578 monument at Dartington, but not all have been accounted for - certainly not all the sons at any rate. There are at least two unnamed younger sons still to be identified, and it is thus natural to suspect that here we would find the two missing names. One or two histories and pedigrees of the Champernowne family, especially that by C.E.Champernowne in 1954, are fairly comprehensive but not exhaustive. Even that family researcher had failed to identify all of Sir Arthur Champernowne's children.

In *Acts of Privy Council*:

At Croidon [?Croydon, Surrey] Aug 25, 1556. "John Champernone, servant to Wm Knight, one of the Customers of Southampton, understanding that he was sent for from hence, cam this daie and made his personal apparence and desired the same might be recorded."

Could this otherwise unknown John Chapman be a candidate for the one to ultimately go to Kerry?

THE PLANTING OF MUNSTER IN THE 1580s

Having now to a certain extent determined the Chapman (alias Champernowne) early origins, and their relationship to Ralegh, attention now turns to the Irish connection. Firstly, it is necessary to consider the circumstances under which they and Ralegh would have found themselves in Ireland in the late 1500s.

In June 1998, enquiries were initiated there, whilst other appropriate lines of research continued to be started in the U.K.

The earlier invaders of Ireland, the Anglo-Norman nobles, had gone almost completely Irish, out of a natural instinct of self-preservation. The English 'Pale' had contracted to a strip of some 20 miles west and north of Dublin, being the richest, most settled and civilised part of the country, and consisting essentially of the counties of Dublin, Louth and Meath. 'The Pale' describes the area of Ireland, centred around Dublin. that was ruled by the English in the Middle Ages. The term came from the Latin word *palum*, meaning stake. At its height The Pale consisted of Dublin, Louth, Meath, Kilkenny, Tipperary and Wexford. The Irish living outside this area of English jurisdiction were said to be "beyond the Pale", a saying still in common use today. Beyond the Pale the English and Irish intermixed, with a common religion. However, the English were generally against any Irish rebellion.

In 1541 Henry VIII took on the additional title of King of Ireland, and the country began to become more Anglicised with English laws and customs. He also made himself head of the Church instead of the Pope, who had refused him a divorce from Queen Catherine. Ireland had its own language and culture, traditions and customs, living in a different world. There was thus a liability for a natural clash between the two, resulting in some opposition, and even rebellion. As well also of the continuous undercurrent of different religions (Anglican *v* Roman Catholic), for with the accession of Edward VI in 1547 Protestantism became the official religion instead of Catholicism, which changed back again with the accession of

Mary in 1553. Then in 1558 it changed yet once more with the accession of Protestant Elizabeth.

Gaelic was spoken throughout Ireland until the 16th century, but declined as the English increased their hold over the country, and imposed their own language and customs.

During this period there were three serious rebellions in Ireland. Firstly was that of Shane O'Neill in Ulster in the 1550s-1560s, which was finally quashed. Then came the two Desmond Rebellions in Munster during the period from 1568 until November 1583 when the Earl of Desmond was killed.

During Mary's reign there had been some clearing of the native tribes from whole districts by expulsion or extermination, to make room for English and Scottish settlers. Plantations were attempted in Ulster and mid-Ireland, but the natives resisted such that from the beginning the settlers had to fight for their lives and for their newly acquired possessions, aided by government forces. Despite atrocities against the natives by the planters the two schemes more or less failed.

Late 16th century Colonial experimenters from Devon were St.Leger, Grenville, Ralegh, with the career of Humphrey Gilbert as Colonel of forces in Munster. All these were in some way inter-related, and thus with the Champernownes. Whilst in England, in November 1566, Gilbert was in touch with his West Country relations who were interested in the idea of planting Ulster. Queen Elizabeth sent him back in July 1567 with power to negotiate with the Lord Deputy (Lord Grey of Wilton) on behalf of

certain gentlemen of the West parts of England

about the plantation.

20 July 1567 correspondence in *Calendar of State Papers-Ireland (CSPI)* from Sir William Cecil to Lord Deputy Sydney as being in favour

of the bearer Sir Arthur Champernowne, repairing to have conference with Humfrey Gylberte relative to intended plantation.

Gilbert's and the West Country's interests were then to shift to the southern province of Ireland – Munster. St.Leger, and his partner/kinsman Richard Grenville, (Grenville had married a St.Leger cousin), had brought across a small number of Devon men, and began to settle and break in their Munster lands. There was a resultant rebellion by the local Irish, backed by Spain, and all these first settlement lands were to be lost.

Champernowne, the head of that family at Dartington in Devon, was the uncle of the three Gilberts and Ralegh, and cousin of the Grenvilles and St.Legers. Ralegh, born c.1552, in 1572 started at Oriel College, Oxford with one of his Champernowne kinsman.

1568-1573 was the period of the First Desmond Rebellion in Ireland.

1572 In 'Humphrey Gilbard's [?Gilbert's] Report – The discourse of Ireland', he said that only the $^1/_5$ part was inhabited by Englishmen. The land was more chargeable than profitable. Waste ground was offered by the Queen to Sir Arthur Champernowne and Sir Humphrey Gilbert. (*Carew MSS, Vol. 1, 1515-1574*) See 1583.

5 October 1572 Sir Arthur Champernowne in a letter to Queen Elizabeth offered to find volunteers for the French wars, stating that Devon could supply over sixty

younger brothers to gentillmen, meane gentillmen being heyres, franklins and other lusty young felos all unmarried the worst of them having iij annuities and other yerely profits – xx^{li}.

These 'gentillmen' were thus to include members of an extended family containing Walter Ralegh the younger, presumably the two young Champernownes/Chapmans, and Edward Denny, who were to serve under Arthur, Lord Grey of Wilton, the Lord Deputy of Ireland and related to Denny by marriage. *The Kerry Magazine* of 1 September 1854 contained a long article about Sir Edward Denny (later of Tralee in co. Kerry), which included his family connections:

Burleigh, the Prime Minister, was his [Denny's] near connexion by the marriage of the Earl's daughter, Lady Anne Cecil, with his namesake and nephew, Edward Lord Denny, - Sir Francis Walsingham the able Secretary of State to Elizabeth, was his cousin-german on the father's side, as were maternally Walter Rawleigh, and John and William Chapman, the original grantees of the large Kerry estates now possessed by the Earl of Cork, and families deriving under him.

Denny was son of one of Henry VIII's courtiers, and a cousin to Ralegh and Sir Humphrey Gilbert, plus first cousin to Sir Francis Walsingham. The mother of Walsingham (c.1530-1590) was the daughter of Sir Edmund Denny. Walsingham had been M.P. for Lyme Regis in Dorset, on the border with Devon, from 1563 to 1567. He was ambassador to France 1570-1573, and then Secretary of State for foreign affairs until his death. Walsingham in catholic France was probably instrumental in the English force sent to France in 1572. He was an ardent protestant, and was energetic in pursuing the protection of Huguenots in France and the Low Countries. Lord Burghley was afterwards to be related by marriage.

July 1579. James Fitzmaurice, a cousin of the Earl of Desmond led a small invasion force in Spanish ships that landed at Dingle, and subsequewntly burned the town. But he was to be killed in a skirmish with another cousin when on his way to rally disaffection in the north, in what was to become the Second Desmond Rebellion. (See 10 November 1580)

11 July 1580. The Privy Council appropriated to Ralegh and Edward Denny £100 each. On 15 July one hundred of the City of London's quota of three hundred soldiers for service in suppressing the Munster rebellion were to be put under the command of Ralegh, and another hundred under Denny. The retribution meted out to the Irish rebels was barbaric by civilised modern-day standards, with hangings sometimes followed by drawing and quartering. This was considered acceptable at that time, by the English at any rate, though naturally causing revulsion amongst the Catholics of Spain and Rome. Walsingham could well have recommended his kinsmen Ralegh and Denny for

this venture to Ireland.

25 August 1580 At Cork, in southern Ireland, although George Carew managed to escape, Sir Peter Carew was murdered in an ambush by the Irish, in retaliation for the killing by Ralegh and Sir Wareham St.Leger of Sir James Fitzgerald. He was one of the many early English settlers who had gone native Irish.

10 November 1580 Ralegh was soon able to avenge the death of his kinsman Carew. At Dún an Óir on the western side of Smerwick Harbour, on the small cliff promontory, Piers Rice had built a 'perty castel' about a year before, with an outer wall on the landward side, cutting off a tongue of land which drops to the sea below. According to McMorran this had previously been an Iron Age fort. The garrison there consisted of some beseiged some 200 Irish, and about 400 Spanish, Italian and Basque mercenaries (though other reports say 700 Spanish, etc.) They had arrived by sea in the September under the papal flag, to help James Fitzmaurice strengthen the Desmond Rebellion against the English crown. Before additional fortifications could be completed they were attacked on the 7th by a force under Lord Deputy Grey de Wilton and the Earl of Ormond, and with Admiral Sir William Winter's fleet blockading the harbour. The siege only lasted three days, when the garrison's Spanish general surrendered, and begged for mercy, although well provisioned with food and ammunition. After some officers had been put aside for ransom, Captains Ralegh and Mackworth were sent into the fort, who then

entered into the castle, and made a great slaughter, many or most part of them being put to the sword,

Fitzmaurice was apparently amongst those so slaughtered. The Spanish and Italians were put to the sword, the Irish were hanged. Prisoners were not to expect fair treatment in those days, and this particular incident was not exceptional. It would seem most possible that one, if not both 'Chapmans/Champernownes' may well have been involved in this incident.

The 1986 *Dingle Peninsula Archaeological Survey* by Cuppage *et al* contains a contemporary description and plan of the fort, being on a small oval promontory some 30 metres x 25 metres, enclosed by a stone rampart, the approach to which was defended by a deep narrow causeway spanned by a drawbridge. To visit the site now is to be somewhat disappointed. Only part of the rampart remains, with outlines of other landward defence banks, earthworks, and bastions enclosing a triangular area 30 metres x 40 metres x 40 metres. It is difficult to now visualise that number of people encamped on such a relatively small area. Smith in 1756 would have seen more of the fortifications. There may have inevitably been undermining and erosion by the sea in the intervening 400 years. There is now a large modern carved monument to the event nearby.

The name Dún an Óir (fort of gold) has erroniously said to be because of the quantity of gold brought by the Italian/Spanish expedition, and buried within the fort. But O'Sullivan's history says the point of land was so named before their arrival. Natives called it 'The Golden Port', or as the point of land is indifferently called, the protruding gold mine, washed by the waves, is really bright copper pyrites, which shine and sparkle in the sun. "All that glitters is not gold."

Before this, (according to 'Antiquities of the Barony of Corkaguiny' in *The Kerryman* of 5 November 1927), whilst possibly on their way to Dún an Óir, at

Castlegregory Castle [on the west shore of Tralee Bay]...the poet Spenser, Walter Raleigh, Capt. Zouch and Capt. Denny were entertained by Hugh Hoare, who stabbed his wife to death because she preferred to waste the wine in the cellar rather than give it to the 'Saxon Churls', and who himself fell dead as he was being escorted for trial...

Edmund Spenser (c.1552-1599) had as patron the Earl of Leicester, on whose behalf he possibly first came to Ireland in 1577. In 1580 he became secretary to Lord Deputy Grey de Wilton, and both came to Ireland the same year. Spenser was to remain in Ireland, except for two brief visits to England, until the close of 1598 and within a month of his death. He accompanied Wilton to Kerry in November 1580, and was to be present at the taking of Smerwick castle. The time spent in Kerry, and scenes witnessed, permanently depressed him and blighted his attitude to the Irish. In 1581 he was to be appointed clerk of the Irish court of chancery, which post he was to hold for seven years. He also received and sold leases, and eventually resided at New Abbey in co. Kildare. He suffered financial difficulties for the best part of his life.

12 May 1581 In a letter from Lord Deputy Grey to Walsingham *CSPI*, it was reported that a

Barry Roe [red-headed Barry] who killed George Chapman is protected, and David Barry is proclaimed.

C. E. Champernowne wrote in 1954 that a George Champernowne had been 'slain in Ireland'. He had earlier been mentioned in the Will of his father Sir Arthur Champernowne.

Autumn 1581 As Ireland was now somewhat quieter, Ralegh and his company were returned to England

7 December 1582, at Dublin Castle a Thomas Chapman was clerk of the auditor Jenyson. (Letters to Lord Burghley, etc.)

The Desmond rebellion or war had turned Munster into a desert, where there was now famine and pestilence as all food had been destroyed. Edmund Spenser in his *View of the Present State of Ireland*, written in 1596 after over fifteen years in that country, described in appalling terms the miseries of those peasants who had survived. Not only the English operated a kind of scorched-earth policy, but the Irish sometimes destroyed crops and even houses to deprive the English of the use of them. (*CSPI 1592-1596*, pages 335 and 343). This mostly adversely affected the native Irish of course, as Spenser stated:

Notwithstanding that the same (Munster) was a most rich and plentiful country, full of corn and cattle, that you would have thought they would have been able to stand long, yet ere one year and a half they were brought to such wretchedness, as any stony heart would have rued the sight. Out of every corner of the woods and glyns [glens] they came creeping forth upon their hands, for their legs could not bear them; they looked like anatomies of death, they spake like ghosts crying out of their graves; they did eat of the dead carrions, happy were they if they could find them, yea, and one another soon after, insomuch as the very carcasses they spared not to scrape out of their graves; and if they found a plot of watercresses or shamrocks, there they flocked as to a feast for the time, yet not able long to continue there withal: that in short space there were none almost left, and a most populous and plentiful country suddenly made void of man and beast.

There were said to be instances of cannibalism, particularly of very young children; and packs of wolves would attack the weak - including adults.

c.1583 In the *Carew MSS, Vol. 2, 1575-1588*:

'The coming to me thither [Carrickfergus] of Sir Arthur Champernowne, Mr Henry Champernowne, his eldest brother's son and heir, Mr Philip Butside [Budockshed], and divers other gentlemen, yeomen, and seamen of the west of England, desirous to take lands and to inhabit in the north parts of Ireland [Ulster].'

Philip Budockshed was said to have died this same year at Carrickfergus, without leaving any children.

Grenville, as Colonel of the army in Munster, had by now eventually suppressed the rebellion. On 11 November 1583 the Earl of Desmond, leader of the rebellion was eventually captured by a party of hostile Irish, and beheaded by one Daniel Kelly, with the head being sent to London for public display. The body was temporarily buried at Glounageenth, but finally buried at Kilnaruma - but see TIRRILASIGHAGHIE in Chapter 6. Desmond's extensive lands in Munster were seized for the Crown. Although Munster itself was now in a terrible plight it provided the biggest opportunity, so far, for planting, as some half a million acres were declared forfeit by the rebellious treason.

8 January 1584. Kilkenny. In the *CSPI 1574-85*, page 488, *SP/63/107/13* is a note by the Earl of Ormond:

The ward [or guard] at Castlemaigne discharged by one Champion.

This castle at Castlemaine (Caislean na Mainge) had been built c.1215 over the Maine River, a few miles south of Tralee in co. Kerry, and was shown on a 1572 map depicting the siege of that date. (PRO *MPF78*) The castle was demolished by General Ludlow in the troubles of 1641 after its capture from the Irish, though remains existed certainly into the 1800s. The old bridge itself was completely demolished in the 20th century, and thus all signs of the castle have gone.

Below is a representation of the castle copied from an engraving in *Pacata Hibernia*, as it was in 1600, and reproduced in Bary's *Houses of Kerry*.

In 1584 a Parliamentary commission was appointed to survey the immense area of Munster, and although not able to do a complete survey it was to reveal the fragmented extent of escheated land and the haphazard nature of confiscation of the late Earl of Desmond's properties. It was Burghley's intention to exploit them.

As Ranger's thesis says:

Ireland offered opportunity of forfeiture, resumption and extension of the claims of the crown to Irish land, and of the financial exploitation of feudal tenure, It also offered possibilities of profitable royal investment in recovered agriculture and industry.

December 1585- a scheme for peopling (or planting) Munster was drawn up.

The escheated lands were to be re-peopled by English settlers.

The offered seignories were to be of 12,000 - 8,000 - 6,000 - 4,000 acres. No undertaker was supposed to have more than 12,000 acres. For a full seignory the undertaker had to settle 91 families including his own - 6 freeholders, 6 farmers, 42 copyholders, and 36 base tenures and cottagers. (*CSPI 1586-88*, pages 84-89, *SP/63/124/95*)

Freeholders were to have 300 acres each, farmers 400 acres, copyholders 100 acres, and the remainder 50 - 20 - 10 acres at the discretion of the undertaker. Other size seignories were to be in proportion. Freeholders and farmers were expected to dispose of £70.7s.0d each, copyholders £28.16s.8d, cottagers £6.4s.8d. Over half this outlay was on stock.

Undertakers had to accomplish this settlement in seven years, i.e. by Michaelmas 1593. Seignories were to be run similar to the English manor system, with courts leet and courts baron.

A militia system was also to be set up, to provide an element of defence for each seignory. From Michaelmas 1590 every undertaker himself had to provide three horsemen and six footmen, all fully furnished. Freeholders and farmers had each to provide one equiped horseman. Every copyholder of 100 acres was to have equipment for one footman. Thus the total force for each seignory of 12,000 acres (around 25 square miles) should have come to 15 horsemen and 48 foot. In the meantime defence would be provided by garrisons, at Crown expense.

December 1585. In 'A Note of the Benefit that may grow in short time to the younger Houses of Gentlemen [in

England] by this course, in perpetuity, taking the greatest Portion in the Plot' it was proposed:

The gentleman undertaker to be the chief lord of so great a seigniory or parish, and to have the "manrode" (homage) of so many families, and the disposing of so many good holdings, as the greatest portion set down in Her Majesty's plot doth offer, is a thing fit for gentlemen of good behaviour and credit, and not for any man of inferior calling. To have the royalties and perquisites of courts within the whole, will be no doubt, a matter of good benefit to him in time to come, then to have £100 *per annum* clear of revenue, to be paid yearly, as the Queen's Majesty's rent is paid, and yet with good content to the taker, is a thing very easy to be performed; besides, the profit that he may make of his own demesne with the first year, with a reasonable stock, as is set down, may prove to be worth (*blank*), the second year more; and after the same shall come to full manurance, is very likely to prove worth (*blank*) *per annum* at the least; and surely considering the smallness of the charge which groweth, even in the first year, which is the greatest year of burden; and withal that a great part of the money required in the same, doth still remain to himself in stock, beside many other commodoties, which the nature and fertility of that soil may bear, must needs prove this course very beneficial to the undertaker, if the same shall be well pursued, and effectually dealt in, and that he doth enter into the same with due consideration, as is meet...
It is to be considered, the first year's charge overpassed, he may have the second year, corn and cattle sufficient for him and his family to spend, whereby he may be at no charge, by reason of necessary expenses in his household, that second year; and the third year, he will have to spare both corn, cattle, work, etc., which he may [find] a vent for at all times, either into England or other countries to his great benefit. (*Desiderata Curiosa Hibernica* by J. Lodge, 1772)

Thus in February 1586 letters were sent to Justices in Cornwall, Devon, Dorset, Somerset and Cheshire, for interested gentlemen

of good family

and sufficient means.

14 February 1586 the following letter of the Privy Council was sent to certain "Somersetshire Gentlemen":

Her Majesty has entered into consideration of some plot for the repeopling of such parts of Munster in Ireland, as are now in her possession. The plot offers many advantages to the younger children, brethren and kinsfolk of gentlemen of good families, and to those of inferior calling and degrees. We therefore have made choice of you to treat with such of that county of Somerset as you find able and willing to accept of and undertake the same, and have given order to John Popham, Esq., Attorney-General [of England], to confer with you therein. (*Cal. Carew MSS.*, II. 419)

Dorset, Somerset, Devon, Lancashire and Cheshire seem to have been specially, but not exclusively favoured by such soliciting letters, but targetted as being nearest to Ireland, and between which there was already inter-communication. Leicestershire thus does not seem to have been specifically mentioned, or canvassed.

There was a syndicate of Devon and other counties' members, largely outside the west, and linked by connections other than county residence. Their leader was a Southampton merchant, Henry Oughtred, being granted Mayne in co. Limerick. His application in May 1586 numbered 18 men, willing to take 15½ seignories, a total of 186,000 acres. They proposed to settle in Connello and Kerry. Two of their number were Sir Valentine Browne of Middlesex and Lincolnshire, with Molahiffe in co. Kerry, and Sir William Herbert of Montgomeryshire with Castleisland in co. Kerry, who later detached themselves before June to form a different group to settle Kerry alone (*CSPI 1574-85, SP/63/124/87*) - see below. Their associates at this early stage were still unknown. Among those at Court who did their duty and took up lands on a large scale were Sir Christopher Hatton of Northants with Knocknamona in co. Waterford, and Ralegh. Among those who had West Country connections were Sir Wareham St. Leger of Kent with Carrigaline in co. Cork; Sir William Courtenay of Devon with Newcastle in co. Limerick, Francis Berkeley of Somerset with Askeaton in co. Limerick; and Sir George Bourchier of Devon, with Logh Gur in co. Limerick.

17 June 1586 According to a map described in the *CSPI, MPF273*, those undertakers mentioned as being at Youghall in Inchiquin, co. Cork, were Sir Walter Rawley, Carew Rawley, Richard Champernown, and --Chydley - all kinsmen of one sort.

21 June 1586 The earlier plantation scheme was amended in 'An Abstract of the Articles for repeopling and inhabiting the Province of Munster in Ireland.' (*CSPI*, pages 84-89) It was finally decided how these seized lands were to be settled, in what was to be known as the Munster Plantation, with the enterprise being strongly supported by Queen Elizabeth.

There were 86 potential undertakers in all - nine were knights, two the eldest sons of knights, seven more sons of knights, 39 styled esquires and 22 gentlemen. The main Kerry undertaker was Edward Denny.

Army, or ex-army men, (sometimes referred to as servitors,) officials and others on Crown service in Ireland could also qualify as undertakers. The army ones' claim for grants of the escheated land was a strong one, backed by three considerations: the continuous shortage of money to pay arrears, previous government promises, and the servitors' own position as custodees of portions of the confiscated land since 1582. By early 1586 there were six or so military men with assurances of grants from the escheated land, and more had petitioned for land as yet with no success.

Sir William Herbert and Sir William Browne had dispatched a vanguard of 50-60 English persons to take possession in Kerry, before the survey commissioners and measurers had started their business in midsummer 1587. So they may have gained some sort of possession, as at least three of the Kerry undertakers, Herbert, Conway and Denny were personally in residence in early 1587. All plantation lots were in possession by 1588.

How did the Elizabethans see Ireland? It was in a state of arrested development: still being mediæval, which the Renaissance had passed by, and having been left behind by a world that had gone on without her. It was a primitive world of incessant fighting on a small scale - fought with battle-axes that had been the latest thing in the Norse period. Literature had stood still for 300 years. The Elizabethans were shocked. There were ample natural resources which were just not being exploited by the 'native' population. There had been attempts at colonisation, when the Irish had been driven off their land, but the abortive settlements had the colonists driven out by the Irish who moved back in. But in the end the Elizabethans did subdue Ireland, and an integration and fusion of peoples was ready to begin. Then came the English Civil War of the 1640s, and all hopes of this integration were to be dashed.

Edmund Spenser was to say in his possibly exaggerated and biased *View of the Present State of Ireland*, that that country was

a nation ever acquainted with wars, though but amongst themselves, and in their own kind of military discipline trained up ever from their youths,

Nothing could restrain the fury of Irish broils:

...whensoever they make head, no laws, no penalties, can restrain, but that they do in the violence of that fury tread down and trample underfoot all, both divine and human, things...There are two sorts of people in Ireland to be considered of; the one called the Kerne, the other the Churls, The Kerne bred up in idleness and naturally inclined to mischiefs and wickedness, the Churl willing to labour and take pains, if he might peaceably enjoy the fruits thereof,

Spenser approved of this Planting, and in 1588 became clerk of the council of Munster. He was to be granted 3,028 acres in co. Cork, where was now to live.

The Elizabethans conceived their efforts as being to help and advance the interests of the churls, the simple people at the bottom; and they would have achieved this, if only they could have got across the barriers made by race, language and religion. The manners and customs were those of a pastoral society much on the move, particularly in summer when the whole community with their cattle moved up into the mountains or into the wilds. These habits were conducive to thieving and encouragement of outlaws.

Cattle were the chief currency. There was very little money anywhere in Ireland, with some payments even being made in Spanish ducats.

All was still primitive and raw. The habit of wearing glibs - a thick mass of hair over their eyes - made disguise easy, detection difficult: hence the constant legislation against the wearing of glibs and long Irish mantles (in which weapons were easily concealed) and the efforts to enforce English dress. The Irish had the manners of the Dark Ages. Their dwellings were

rather swine-sties than houses...the chiefest cause of his so beastly manner of life and savage condition, lying and living together with his beast in one house, in one room, in one bed.

It has been said in extenuation that animals were possibly brought into the house for shelter, as to provide separate sheds and the like for them could involve the tenants in additional rent; plus, the animals would provide additonal warmth in winter-time.

Barnabe Rich, an Essex gentleman, ardent Protestant, author of many popular tracts, having by 1612 lived for many years in Ireland, was described then as:

Barnabie Rych Gent, Servant to the King's Most Excellent Majesty

in his *A New Description of Ireland* was still more outspoken about Irish husbandry and manners. The Irish would

rather still retain themselves in their sluttishness, in their uncleanliness, in their rudeness...than they would take any example from the English, either of civility, humanity or any manner of decency.

People all over Ireland

had no other means to draw the plough but every ox by his own tail;...

When the hair of the tail was rubbed so short it could no longer be tied, the plough stood still. Even about Dublin the hay-harvest was left over till the corn-harvest, with the result that much of it was ruined by rain. If the Irish were not so lazy and cultivated their land better, it would sustain a much higher population. There was room for plenty of English to come in and improve things, but the natives would rather keep things as they were and occupy themselves in preying upon their audacious improvers. The Irish held it unlucky to keep their milking vessels clean, so that they were most filthily kept.

I myself have seen that vessel which they hold under the cow...to be furred half an inch thick with filth.

Dublin was served with the loathsome butter. Irish washing was worse, and smelt worse. Rich further observed:

...myself have seen a woman sitting with a mustard quern between her bare thighs grinding of oatmeal, I think a man would have little list to eat of the bread. But of this meal as ill in complexion to look upon as a little dirt under a man's feet they make their cakes, for other bread they have none and it is but seldom when they have this...the farmers of Ireland are far to seek in many points of husbandry and the women (for the most part) have as little skill of housewifery.

But on the other hand there was a great resort to charms, spells, enchantments, etc., and a universal addiction to fasting on fast-days, to holy wells, relics and pilgrimages. It could therefore be understood why there was the insistence on the planting of Munster being solely by English settlers.

There was of course a more positive side to the above perceived Irish character. In the 15th and 16th centuries , there were flourishing private schools in various parts of the country for Law, Medicine, History, Literature, Classics, and poetry. Libraries (of books dating from the 5th or 6th century) had been formed in monasteries, colleges and private homes, though many of these libraries were to be destroyed or scattered during the several troubled times. Irish scholars and missionaries greatly helped to spread learning and religion all over England and the Continent. There was the Brehon law, under which offenders had to atone for injuries to persons or property by a compensation payment. This Brehon code followed that as originally followed by the Anglo-Saxons, Franks, Germans, and Greeks. Anglo-Norman colonists of Ireland were to adopt this code.

To provoke the English more, there was the natural wit and conversation of the Irish. Then they were a good-looking people, especially the women. Finally, there was the beauty of the landscape, of which Spenser was to especially mention that of Munster.

A. L. Rowse in his *The Expansion of Elizabethan England* was uncertain whether the Irish were anti-English because they were Catholics, or whether they remained Catholics because they were anti-English.

Thus although there has been some further substantiation for believing the name of Champernowne becoming Chapman, no mention had been found so far of a John and William.

JOHN CHAPMAN'S LAND GRANTS IN KERRY

Anyone making enquiries relating to pre-modern Ireland should know of course that such is beset with problems. A great many of the valuable Irish national archival records that had been deposited at the central judiciary Four Courts building in Dublin were destroyed during 'The Troubles' of 1922. Apparently the Republican Irregulars at the beginning seized the building on 28 June, the Free State artillery opened fire on them, and they surrendered on the 30th, with civil war following. But during the siege by government forces a great many records inevitably became damaged or destroyed, particularly by fire. According to King those destroyed records included the parish registers of Kerry back to at least 1713. Also, there had been an earlier equally disastrous fire which destroyed the Council Office in Dublin in 1711, when again many papers were lost. These losses naturally cause consequent potential research difficulties. Fortunately some of these records had earlier been copied in full or as extracts, with many such copies being published. Also, quite a number of old records were still with parishes, in private collections, or other Irish and U.K. archives. Thus it is not quite such a daunting research prospect as might at first be expected.

The National Archives at Dublin are unable to provide distance postal research facilties, but a subsequent unexpected visit by the writer to Ireland late in 1999 overcame this difficulty. Fortunately County Record Offices, and Local History and Genealogical Centres, in the Republic of Ireland can generally be most accommodating in accessing and providing useful sources of information, though not all bother to reply to postal enquiries. One explanation offered for the latter is that the Irish do not wish to offend by being unable to help, and therefore having to give negative answers. There are also the many contemporary primary documents in private as well as public depositories outside of Ireland, the custodians of which can be very helpful, and with modest cost for any possible photocopying.

[May] 1582. Sir Francis Walsingham had sent some money to a Mr Champernon at Toulouse. Walsingham, as part of his duties of responsibility for foreign affairs, had built up one of the most comprehensive network of spies and informants to protect the Queen Elizabeth's interests, and this could well have been a payment for such services rendered. (*CSP Domestic*)

Although Queen Elizabeth had given Ralegh the wealth to form a settlement in The New World, she did not allow him to accompany the colonising party in 1585 under Sir Richard Grenville, who was related to him by marriage with the St.Legers of Bideford. A colony was started at Roanoke Island, in what was later to be named Virginia (after Elizabeth). A relief fleet under Ralegh's kinsman Sir Francis Drake went there in 1586, but the colonists requested to be brought home. Ralegh's own fleet, again under Grenville, arrived a couple of weeks later. Finding nobody at Roanoke, Grenville left just a small party to guard the settlement until a new body of colonists would arrive. The party was under the command of two Barnstable mariners, Coffin and Chapman (christian names not known), and who were all soon to be murdered by local Indians, etc. A colony was finally established there in 1587.

29 August 1586. That there were Chapmans in Ireland during the Elizabethan period has already been shown, though not necessarily recently derived from Devon. In *CSPI Vol. 125, No. 67*, in a letter of this date from Wallop in Dublin to Lord Burghley, mention is made of a Thomas Chapman, who had "long served Mr Auditor" as Clerk of Auditor in Ireland. (See 7 December 1582 in Chapter 3)

The *IGI* gives a Cecily/Cicily Champernon/Champernowne as having married [Sir] Simon Flemming of Slane at Meath in 1355. She seems to have been the only daughter of Sir Thomas and Eleanor (née Rohart/Rohaud)

December 1586. Clerk of the Auditor, Thomas Chapman was petitioning for new post(s).

According to King 'in 1586 a Cornelius Champion was granted the Ferriter or Blasquet islands [off the west end of the Dingle Peninsula], afterwards purchased by Sir Richard Boyle.' Unfortunately nothing else is known of any

Cornelius Champernowne/Champion/Chapman. See also under DOURKYNE in Chapter 6.

31 January 1587. Sir N. White, Master of the Rolls in Dublin, wrote to Burghley that Clerk of the Auditor

Thomas Chapman hath painfully deserved his wages.

18 April 1587. This same Thomas Chapman is said to have served Auditor Jengson 20 years, and possibly was now to be employed elsewhere.

Ralegh's Irish lands were held in co. Cork, on the south coast, and the supposed Chapman lands in co. Kerry in the south-west - both being part of the southern province of Munster. Enquiries were thus made of both counties, with varying degrees of helpfulness. Most advantageously it was to be from the Libraries Section of Kerry County Council. From there it was learned of the published two books of *Selections from Old Kerry Records* in 1872 and 1874, by Mary Agnes Hickson. She is considered by the Kerry County Library as a highly regarded genealogist and historian.

In writing about Sir Edward Denny, who was another large grantee in co. Kerry, Mary Hickson stated that John and William Chapman were Ralegh's maternal cousins-german. Thus whilst she had noted the 'maternal' link omitted from more recent editions of *Burke*, she unfortunately did not give specific family-tree details to show this connection.

Early in this study it became apparent that two important sources of Munster Plantation history were publications by David B. Quinn in 1966, and Michael MacCarthy-Morrogh in 1986. Whilst both gave useful background details of the whole Munster Plantation saga of the late 16th-early 17th centuries, neither initially helped the John Chapman search. However, on obtaining a copy of MacCarthy-Morrogh's Ph.D. thesis of 1983 on which his subsequent book was based, matters took a turn for the better, though he had been unable to actually determine Stone's and Champion's origins. It was from his thesis that much of the following information was derived.

May 1587. A certificate for 8,000 acres was awarded to Thomas Heyford, Ambrose Lacy, George Stone and John

Champion. Apparently possession was delivered to Lacy in July 1587. (*CSPI* page 235. *SP/63/131/6*) Other than Stone and Champion the origins of the others are apparently unknown. This seignory was mostly on the Dingle peninsula in Kerry, in the barony of Corkaguiny: plus a small portion at Ballymacdonnell (after which the seignory was named) between Castleisland and Currans.

19 December 1587. Lacy was soon excluded in favour of Stone, which earned Lacy's protests but little else. (*SP/63/132/40*).

For a year or two after the Armada (1588) Ralegh and Gilbert were the most active and energetic of the undertakers in Munster. Ralegh took up some 12,000 acres in county Cork to begin with, and started to bring over West Country settlers. Also in county Cork, Grenville took up again his partnership with St.Leger; and by May 1589 he had brought over 99 settlers, St.Leger 46. A number of Grenville's family circle accompanied him: his second son John; his half-brother John Arundell; two brothers-in-law John Bellew and Thomas Stukeley; and Christopher Harris who became his son-in-law.

Amongst the land grants was the following, according to Hickson's *Old Kerry Records, 2nd Series*:

By Patent, dated 31st year of Elizabeth [1588-1589], JOHN CHAMPION and GEORGE STONE, Trustees of the Hospital of Ross, county Wexford, had a grant to them and their assigns for ever of the whole barony of Corcaguiny, which was then described as divided into two districts Corcaguiny proper and Litter (*i.e.* Letteragh.) See also 1611.

Before considering the barony of Corcaguiny, or more correctly the seignory of Ballymacdonnell, there is the intriguing question of this Trusteeship of the Hospital of Ross. The town of Ross was in fact New Ross, to differentiate it even then from the nearby and much smaller Old Ross. The following information has been derived from Hore's *History of Wexford*. On the site of St. Saviour's Chapel was founded the Hospital of the Most Holy Trinity, by the bequest of Thomas Gregory, gent. A warrant to which was first recorded in the Fiants of Queen Elizabeth, dated 12 February 1578, with a subsequent grant of a Royal Charter dated 1 September 1587. The administration of the Hospital was by a series of Masters, subject to the consent and advice of the Sovereign and four of the Seniors of the Council of the town. Were Champion and Stone of this latter number? Unfortunately no names were given. The hospital consisted of six houses in Priory Street, for the accommodation of fourteen poor woman, each of whom has two rooms, and an annual allowance of £18 1s. By subsequent Letters Patent the Master, 'Bretheren', and 'Poor Sisters' were granted the two Chapels of St. Saviour's and St. Michael's to perform Divine Worship and service in. Hore's book has a plan of New Ross c.1700, showing the location of Trinity Hospital and St. Saviours's church, with St. Michael's and a cemetery nearby.

Apparently the seignory of Ballymacdonnell had been granted by letters patent on 23 February 1589 to a George Stone and John Champion. Ballymacdonnell consisted of lands on and near the Dingle Peninsula on the west coast of co. Kerry. See illustrated map dated 1589, dedicated to Lord Burghley by one of the Munster plantation surveyors, Francis Jobson. It has been twisted 90° clockwise; and clearly seen marked at the top centre, on the Dingle Peninsula which is almost co-incident with the Corkaguiny barony, is printed 'STON AND CHAMPYON'. Stone was said by Hickson to be one of Queen Elizabeth's footmen. Whilst Champion was said to be an ex-soldier, considered possibly connected with Arthur Champion, a potential undertaker from Devon, and related to Edward Denny, who in turn was related to Ralegh, - but frustratingly again no source details were given. This Arthur Champion, however, again seems suspiciously like the Arthur Champernowne mentioned earlier, and could thus be considered further confirmation of the Champernowne and Chapman connection - being linked phonetically by the names Champion/Champen.

In March 1999 a visit was paid to the Library of The Irish Genealogical Research Society in London, which proved productive. There was a copy of Charles Smith's book *State of the County of Kerry*, published in 1756. Amongst an included list of those granted lands during the reign of Queen Elizabeth were:

To *John Champion*, alias *Chapman*, so called by Moryson, and *John Stone* (neither of whose posterity in the male line remain in this county) 1434 acres, at £23,18s *per annum* crown rent, These lands are now the estate of the Rt, Hon, *John*, earl of *Orrery*, having been purchased by the first earl of *Cork* from *Chapman* and *Stone*, as appears by evidences remaining in the castle of *Lismore*.

John Stone is presumably a mis-notation for the George as previously twice noted.

Fynes Moryson (1566-1630) was a well-known English traveller, and became chief secretary to Lord Mountjoy the Lord Deputy of Ireland 1600-1603, and then in England 1603-1606. Moryson, in the second volume of his *Itinerary* of 1617 concerning his travels through Europe, he deals with the history and topography of Ireland.

What might at first glance be disturbing from the point of view of this study is the statement that there was allegedly no "posterity in the male line remain in this county" of Champion/Chapman. From where did Charles Smith derive his information? Was there any succession in a female line? In any case, Smith was referring to Kerry, and thus a succession in any other county cannot be ruled out.

On the other hand, Hickson in her *Old Kerry Records, 2nd Series* was to say:

According to Smith (*History of Kerry*, page 33) Champion and Stone obtained 1,434 acres in Kerry, The former is said to have been the ancestor of the family of Chapman (Barts) in Meath,

On what authority Smith derived this latter statement Hickson did not explain. MacCarthy-Morrogh thankfully quoted most sources of information in his thesis, and a start was made to check some of them out, in order to verify and seek out other references to Champion or Chapman, though he too equated Champion with Chapman, but without source. Visits were made to the Public Record Office at Kew, principally to copy appropriate original papers listed in the *CSPI* of that period.

One of MacCarthy-Morrogh's sources was another Ph.D. thesis, that of T. O. Ranger in 1959, titled *The Career of Richard Boyle, First Earl of Cork in Ireland 1588-1643*, to whom John Chapman (or whatever he was called) had allegedly sold the county Kerry lands, according to *Burke*.

Ranger was able to show that Boyle had arrived in Ireland in 1588 as a young fortune hunter, with very little to his name - £27, his rapier and dagger. He had been a student at the Middle Temple, in London. Burghley exploited the situation by attempting to stimulate recovery and extension by the mechanism of the grant of concealments - q.v. 'Dictionary of Terms' at the beginning of this work. He was content to allow grantees and officials concerned to make profits, but imposed a series of restrictions which were designed to safeguard the long-term interests of the crown. By 1590 Boyle had been appointed deputy-escheator, with the task of recovering escheated land for the Crown, and arranging their re-lease. He thus achieved a controlling position in the drive for the resumption of determining legal ownership of lands. Between 1590 and 1595 he exploited the drive to his own advantage. He defrauded landowners by falsely alleging concealment and achieving verdicts for the Crown from corrupt juries. He also defrauded grantees by compelling them to sell to him their interest in grants of concealment. In turn he defrauded the Crown by grossly undervaluing the land found, then passing it to himself on grants of concealment and by passing it in reversion at the same rents. Gradually, by these sharp practices he acquired a vast amount of land, - apparently aided and abetted by other officials and adventurers - including John Champen (see 18 July 1597 below).

...as a result of their exploitation of Burghley's drive for resumption its effect was not to benefit the crown, but powerfully to assist the rise of the adventurer class in Ireland.

Boyle obtained more Irish land in 1595 through marriage and further exploitation of his office. Then in 1603/4 he acquired the substantial Raleigh seignories, when the latter fell foul of King James I. The Earl of Cork and Orrery, the present-day successor to the 1st Earl of Cork, was asked whether he had any details of his ancestor's purchase from John Chapman, but apparently any records were now kept largely at Chatsworth House in Derbyshire. Chatsworth confirmed that much of the Lord Boyle archives are kept there, of which some had been published in a somewhat haphazard fashion, but the Keeper of Collections helpfully assisted with researches. Unfortunately late 16th century handwriting can be difficult to read, but clearly decipherable is John Champion's signature on an acquittance to Maurice Stack dated 9 March 1599 - see Chapter 7.

Back on 18 September 1584 the surveying commissioners had left Limerick city to pass over the not particularly high (just over 1,000 feet) Slevelogher hills into Kerry. This route they managed despite atrocious weather, sometimes impassable in wet weather. After viewing central Kerry they made their way with extreme discomfort (according to Wallop - a relation of Ralegh) down the Dingle peninsula to hold an inquisition at Dingle on 6 October, and were back in county Limerick by 16 October. The trip made a deep impression on some of the older members of the commission. Elderly Sir Valentine Browne reported going through "woods, bogs, mountains and dangerous waters" in which some horses drowned. They had to carry all food supplies with them until Dingle was reached for the country could offer them none. (*SP/63/111/90, 112/10, 15 & 18*)

Whilst the rest of northern county Kerry experienced average rainfalls of 40" to 50" a year, the mountains in the Dingle peninsula attracted 60" to 100" or more. Three days of continuous rain in the 1580s - not an unusual occurrence in south-west Ireland - could sever all communications to Kerry. Most of the county's interior is under 250 feet. Two sluggish rivers, the Maigue and the Deel, make their way north from the surrounding high rim to the Shannon estuary.

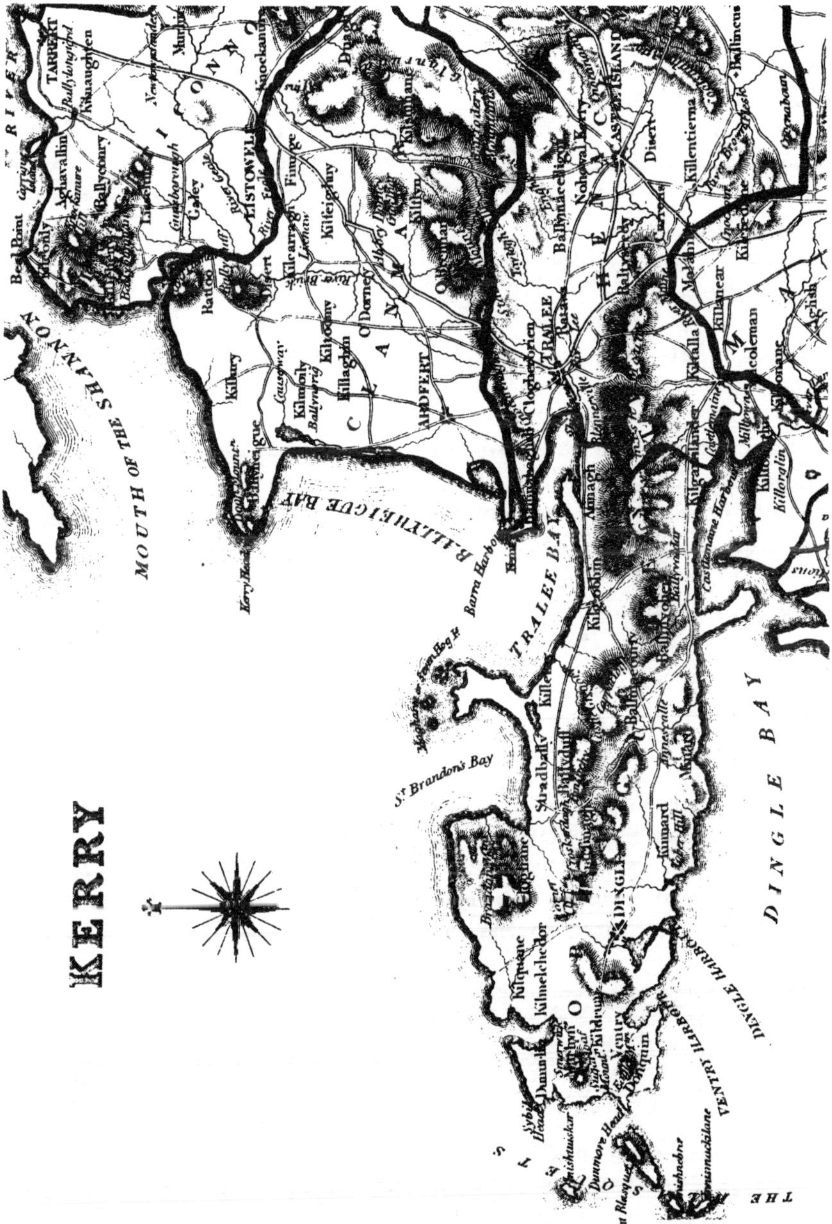
KERRY
MOUTH OF THE SHANNON
BALLYHEIGUE BAY
TRALEE BAY
St Brandon's Bay
DINGLE BAY
VENTRY HARBOUR
DINGLE HARBOUR
Barra Harbor
TRALEE
LISTOWEL
ARDFERT
DINGLE
TARBERT
Kerry Head
Castlemaine Harbor

The region has mostly heavy soils, and the lowlands the lowest rainfall in Munster, 30-40 inches a year. The inadequate drainage, combined with clays, produces a rich grassland ideal for pastoral farming. Scrubby areas were valued at £1.6s.8d.

The 1970 film *Ryans's Daughter* was filmed on the Dingle peninsula, possibly on what were once Chapman lands. It was said that sometimes the prolonged rains held up filming for days.

Kerry in the 1580s in particular was underpopulated, the people being

consumed, what with the sword, and by justice, but chiefly by famine.

The circumstances bringing about this state of affairs can partly be explained by a communication in April 1580 from the Earl of Ormonde to Sir Francis Walsingham, reproduced in *The Kerry Magazine* of 1 September 1854:

The Lord Justice [Sir William Pelham] and I, met near Rathkeale, the 10th of this month, and from thence marched into Kerry, over Slieve-Louchra to Traly [Tralee], - burning, spoiling, and preying the country as we passed; and, coming to Traly, we found the town burning, and the Castel rased by the rebels, and no place left to secure the garrison, but the Abbey, which they left whole. From thence his Lordship and I thought to have gone to the Dingell - being on our waye thitherwarde, word was brought to my Lord, that the Dingel was also rased and burned, and that her Majestie's shippes, (out of which we thought to have had some victuals for our reliefe), were departed to the Harbour of Lymericke.

There may well not have been any (English) population there c.1590.

There were to be frequent land disputes between undertakers, especially in Kerry, through wrongly or incorrectly allocated land as per the letters patent. There was particularly trouble from Sir William Herbert, who was in conflict with many others, including Stone and Champion, with Sir Edward Denny and --Holles also involved - see

CSPI 1586-88, pages 331 & 571; *SP/63/137/31, 31·1; 138/30; 144/56; 145/27; 146/41*).

23 February 1589 Letters patent issued to George Stone and John Champion. (*DKPROI, 16th Report*, page 94, where amount of land not stated, but measured by Francis Jobson in 1586/7 as 1,041 acres in *SP/63/131/59*, or 979 acres in *SP/63/133/96*)

6 March 1589 Sir Edward Denny made a note of Englishmen's lands in Kerry:

Mr Stone, the Queen's footman, and Mr Geford [or Heyford] have taken land of Her Majesty in Kerry, Geford and his wife now dwelling there, (*CSPI 1588-92, page 134; SP/63/141/57*)

The exact extent of these co. Kerry, etc. lands now needed to be determined, but following up references quoted by MacCarthy-Morrogh this was later to be resolved with a productive visit in September 1999 to the National Archives of Ireland in Dublin.

On pages 93-94 of the Appendix to the printed *16th Report of the Deputy Keeper Public Records, Ireland*, 1884, there were transcriptions of Fiants of the Reign of Queen Elizabeth, 1588/9:

5306 Lease (under queen's letter, 29 June, xxx.) to John Champen, gent; of the site of the abbey of Odorney alias our lady abbey of Kyryleison [*Kyrie Eleison*], lands of Clonecanroirke, Dromycomygenyn, Ackrie, and Ballyusin, Boher Roe, Lackimore, Lackybege, and Clonenymetaughe, and Ballibromaine, also the rectory of Odorney, extending to Clonecanroirke, Dromycomygemyn, Ackry, Balliusyn alias Balliusur, Boher Ro, Lackimore, Lackibege, and Clonenymentaugh, also the rectory of Mallahiffe, co. Kerry; the site of the abbey of Rathetowe alias Arragensis, order of S. Augustin, lands in Addergewill, Tirrilaughaghie, and Ardcullen, half the rectories of Liseltin and Gallie, the other half belonging to the vicar there, and a fourth part of the rectory of Aghahamally, co. Kerry; the tithes of the rectories of Ballimanter, Itesbacke, Corbo, Castracar, and Balliamaine, with the chapel and tithes of S. Nicholas in the suburbs of Cork, co. Cork; the chapel of Kilmurry, in Two M'Walter, in the barony of Bealeamo, with land in Kilmurry and Lismohege, co.

Galway; the parcel of land called Monasterie Evan alias Kennett, lying by the town of Higgens, in the barony of Roscoman. To hold for 40 years, from the end of the interests in being. Rent £20.3s. Maintaining 2 English horsemen. Provisions as in 4939. *2 membranes* - [22 Feb.], xxxi. (Auditor General's Patent Book 21, p.17).

5307 Lease (under queen's letter, 29 June, xxx.) to John Champen, gent.; of the site of the house of friars of Timolage, and appurtenances, co. Cork; of the site of the house of friars of the B.V.M. of Kinsale, with appurtenances, co. Cork; and the site of the house of friars of Castellaughan alias Castellian, with appurtenances, co. Cork. To hold for 40 years from the end of the terms in being. Rent £4.10s.2d. Provisions as in 4939 [for English persons only if leased, etc.] -22 Feb., xxxi.

5308 Grant to George Stone and John Champen alias Champion, gentlemen; of the village and butt end of a castle with appurtenances late Bally M'Donnells, lands of M^c^Edmonds, the lands of Dourkyne and Ballyneighe beside Smeerewicke, Menarde, late of Shane m'Edmond M'Ullicke, Farren Edyllhe near Lescache, the two Clonduffs, Glangertarkarrane, and Ballynecorty, late of Morish m'Shane Hussee, the park, a mill (which is to pay to the queen as it shall be valued by the survey), certain lands and tenements in and near Dinglecushe, viz: one house within the town, sometime in the tenure of David Brenaghes, 6s.8d a year, a house with appurtenances there called Ballibradoughe 13s.4d a year, a house between the lands of Stephen Rice, on the north and east and of Thomas M'Gerrot on the south 6s.8d a year, which houses belonged to the said earl in his letting at will, a house and garden in Dingle, late of David duffe Gerrald, attainted, 3s.4d a year, a house with land there, late of John Hussie, slain in rebellion, 10s a year, a burgage and garden late of James Russell, 15s a year, two burgages with a garden there, late of Dominick Fitz Morishe, 10s a year, a tenement there, late of Thomas fitz William ne Boy 5s a year, together with Ballyhe, and all other lands escheated within the trokahid of Corkoneyny, co. Kerry. To hold for ever in fee farm, by fealty, in common socage. Rent, 4d sterling for each English acre which the lands, when surveyed, shall be found to contain, from 1594 (half for preceding 3 years); besides the above named rents in Dingle. Grantees to build houses for 90 families, of which 2 must be for the grantees, 6 for freeholders, 6 for farmers, and 42 for copyholders. With other conditions usual in grants for planting the undertakers in Munster, as in 5302 [i.e. If not built by Michaelmas 1594, the crown may enter, and in final event may be forfeited]. (*2 membranes*, - 23 Feb, xxxi).

Regarding *Fiant 5307*, in 1542, Henry VIII had issued a commission to the Earl of Desmond to dissolve the religious houses of Munster for the King's use. After the Earl's death in 1583, Queen Elizabeth rented the monasteries to various undertakers. In later times they passed into the possession of local landowners, including as we see to John Champen. The ruined monasteries now have no commercial value.

July 1606/1607 Amongst the Crown lands and Tithes in Ireland now in lease from King James I were:

co. Gallway - John Champen, the chapel of Killmurry.
co. Kerry - Assigns of Jo. Champen, lands of the abbey of Ratowth alias Arragacensis, of the order of St Augustin, and of the late abbey of Oderny, alias Ladies Abbey, of Keriolezen [*Kyrie Eleison*].
co. Cork - Jo. Champen, the rectory of Ballinter and Esibacke.
co. Roscommon - Jo. Champen, land near the town of Higgins called Monasterevan alias Kennett late possession of the monastery of Nenaghe [which latter is in co. Tipperary, 19 miles N.E. of Limerick].

Lease of Ballinecourtie, Manegarand, Comeduff, Killgane, Bynnarter & Ballentermon contg CCL acres of land, - stone house newly built. Latiniore & Ballihoa contg CCL acres of land.

Town & lands of Balligahill & Letrynne being of the Mc Edmondes land contg CCCC acres of land, with dwelling house erected upon Balligahill.
Town & lands of Ballinesitor & Churchtowne contg C acres of land and a good house built thereupon.
Part Land of Ballin M^c^Donnell contg C acres, with house built.
Lands of Killalownes part of BallinMcDonnell contg C acres of land & a smaller tenement built thereupon.

Town & lands of Downkyne contg C acres & a small tenement built thereupon,
Town & lands of Ballineigh contg C acres on which a house built,

O'Hart has given the full list of Planters in co. Kerry in the reigns of Elizabeth and James I as: Sir William Herbert, Charles Herbert, Sir Valentine Brown, Sir Edward Denny, John Hollis, Captain Conway, John Champion, George Stone, John Crosbie, Captain Thomas Spring, Stephen Rice (mentioned in *Fiant 5308* above), and Luke Morrice.

Thus there now appears to be yet further substantial and substantiated records of certain lands in co. Kerry being granted to a John Champen/Champion; and a subsequent disposal of these same lands to the Earl of Cork. More circumstantial, but still a strong supposition is that this John Champen/Champion/Chapman was originally a Champernowne. But more of this later after more is found out about these Plantation lands.

1589 map of southern Ireland, showing names of 'STON AND CHAMPYON' top centre, on the Dingle Peninsula

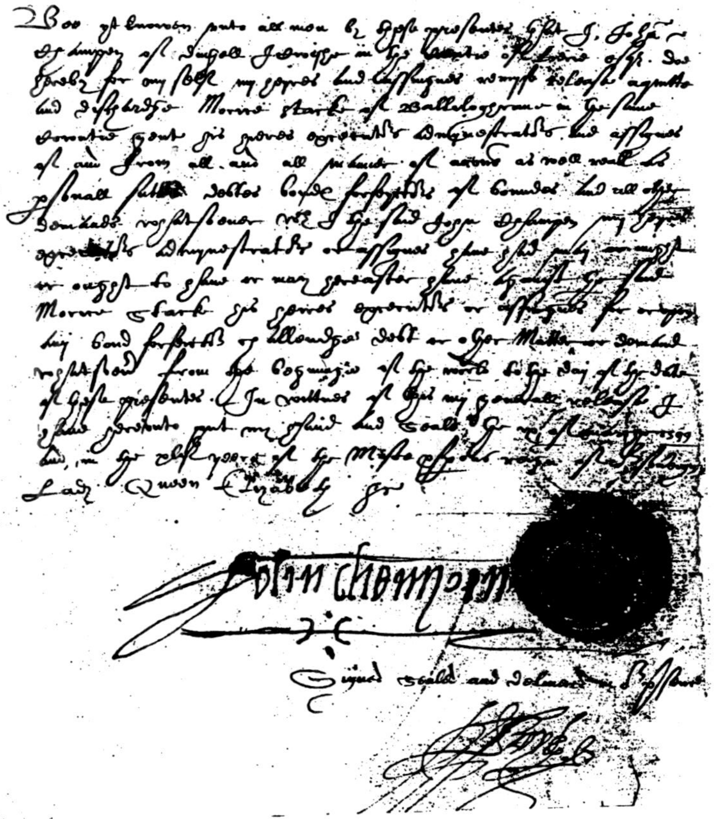

1599 signatures of John Champen and Richard Boyle

Dingle, co Kerry, in the early 1900s

The Champernowne memorial of 1578 in the old church at Dartington.
Does it depict John and William Chapman of Kerry?

DARTINGTON HOUSE,

The Seat of Arthur Champernowne Esqr to whom this Plate is Inscribed

By his Obliged Servant R. Polwhele.

Sir Benjamin Chapman (4th Baronet), and his wife Lady Maria, at the front entrance of Killua Castle, c. 1885.

SIR MONTAGU CHAPMAN, 5TH BART.

Two views of the deteriorating Killua Castle

Ronald Knight, Nancy Lenihan and John Gavin alongside the Sir Walter GRaleigh (sic) obelisk at Killua

South Hill, home of T.E. Lawrence's father, Thomas Robert Tighe Chapman (7th and last Baronet)

THE BARONY OF CORKAGUINY

The barony, as baldly stated by King (*circa* 1925)

> is composed of the parishes of Annagh, Ballinvoher, Bailyduff, Ballynacourty, Cloghane, Dingle, Dunquin, Dunurlin, Garfinny, Kildrum, Kilgobban, Killiney, Kilmalkedar, Kilquane, Kinard, Marhin, Minard, Stradbally, and Ventry. The barony is 24 miles long and eight miles wide; is washed by Dingle and Tralee bays and the ocean which roars on three sides of it; it had a large population formerly; the northern part of the barony is called Litteragh, being coarse and mountainous; it was cultivated to the hill tops in old times, and fenced against wolves until 1710.

But just in what kind of countryside would these Champen/Champion/Chapman seignory land grants and leases have been located within the barony? Something has been seen of how the Dingle Peninsula looked at the time of the Munster Plantation. What of its topography some 400 years later? What remains from that earlier era? One cannot do better than follow David Marshall's *Best Walks in Ireland*.

Dingle Peninsula is the most northerly of the hilly and mountainous promontories, dotted with lakes, which reach out from co. Kerry in the south-western corner of Ireland. It extends westward for more than 30 miles from the low-lying country around Tralee and Killorglin.

It has powerful contrasts of rolling wolds with green fields, gorse hedges, golden beaches and rugged rocks, flat coastal lowlands, blanket bog and angular craggy peaks. Once the home of Brendan the Navigator, the medieval monk who set sail for America in a small leather craft, it is also the site of Garfinny Bridge (Grid Ref: Q 475020), an unmortared stone arch bridge, which may be one of the oldest bridges in Ireland and Britain.

The highest point on the peninsula, Brandon Mountain (3,085 feet), rears up at the end of a chain of hills (often mist/cloud capped or covered), which at Brandon Head plunges almost straight into the sea from a height of 2,462 feet. To the west of this range is a rolling coastal plain studded with typical Irish farms and hamlets. Here there are few stone walls; corn is grown in small square fields, whilst red fuschia hedges, purple-pink foxgloves, pale green ferns, and black moss add their distinctive colourings to the landscape.

This is a Gaelic-speaking area, and old traditions, customs and crafts may still be found very much alive. The area is littered with many prehistoric and Early Christian remains.

The road from Tralee runs west along Tralee Bay to Camp. South-east of the village rises Caherconree (2,668 feet). Beneath the peak stands a massive promontory fort which can be reached by a path off the Camp-Aughils road.

At Camp the R559 road bears south-west and winds its way up through hilly country. In five miles a side road branches off on the left and runs south to Inch, a sheltered seaside resort from which a three mile long ridge of dunes extends into the sea.

4½ miles west, around Anascaul, is an area where wild orchids grow in great variety. The road then continues on its way to Dingle between the hills and the sea. 1½ miles from the little town it passes Ballintaggart, with an old circular burial ground containing a number of ogham stones, some of them with crosses.

Dingle itself, the chief place on the peninsula and the most westerly town in Europe, lies in a sheltered bay with good beaches, surrounded on three sides by hills.

There are many antiquities at the western end of the peninsula. Just west of Dingle, at Milltown, is a large standing stone known as the Milestones, and near this are two others, the Gates of Glory. Continuing west, the road comes to Ventry, 2 miles north-west of which, on the Ballyferriter road, are the ruins of the 15th century Rahinnane Castle, in a circular enclosure surrounded by a moat 30 feet deep.

Then to Ventry Harbour. Ahead is Mount Eagle, from which point onwards there is an area containing within it one of the greatest concentrations of ancient remains in Ireland - *Clochans* (dry stone beehive huts); ogham stones (commemorative Christian gravestones, with inscriptions in the Ogham alphabet, a 4th-5th century adaptation of the

Latin alphabet, originally used for carving inscriptions on sticks), some of them cross-inscribed; promontory forts; ringforts, some of them with souerrains; pillar stones; prostrate stones, one of them with cup-and-circle and other prehistoric markings; cross slabs; ruined churches; oratories; and *bullauns* (stones with a depression in them, probably used as mortars). Unfortunately many of them have been swept away by various agencies.

From Ventry the road follows the rocky south coast. On the left, directly above the sea, along a dangerous path is the fine promontory fort of Dunbeg, with four earthen ramparts and a stone wall. Within the fort are the remains of a house, square in plan within its circular outside wall. An underground passage leads from the interior of the fort to the outside defences.

Nearby, at Glanfahan, is a remarkable group of remains, including 417 beehive huts (built without the use of mortar), 19 souterrains, and 18 standing stones.

The south-western tip of the peninsula is formed by Slea Head, with a sandy shore. The road to Slea Head has been blasted out of the mountainside with explosives. From the narrow road below Mount Eagle (1,695 feet) there are extensive views of the cliffs and the offshore islands. Here is the little fishing harbour of Dunquin, from which boats go out to the Blasket Islands which have had no permanent human habitation since the 1970s.

From Slea Head it is downhill to Coumeenoule Bay, where there is a scattered settlement of about a dozen houses, one of them with a beehive *clochan* standing next to it. These stand on the steep slopes of Mount Eagle, here divided up by stone walls into fields that it has been thought no man would probably ever till again.

At Clogher Head, a rock promontory north of Slea Head, the road turns inland and runs north-east to Ballyferriter. At Reask are the remains of a settlement of hermits.

To the north of Ballyferriter is the broad inlet of Smerwick Harbour, on the west side of which is Dún an Oir, the 'Fort of Gold' (see 10 November 1580 in Chapter 3).

From Ballyferriter a road leads east to Kilmalkedar, one of the most important ecclesiastical sites on the peninsula, where a monastery was founded in the 7th century. In its 12th century Romanesque church is the Alphabet Stone, with ogham and Latin characters side by side. The churchyard has an old sundial, a large monolithic cross, and another ogham stone. 150 yards away is St Brendan's House (15th century), and near this St Brendan's Oratory (see below).

2 miles south-west is the isolated 6th century Gallarus Oratory. Shaped like a perfectly preserved upturned boat (Gallarus = 'strange house'), it has walls over 3 feet thick, so carefully constructed without the use of mortar, that the little chapel (measuring only 15 x 10 feet) is still watertight after 1200 years.

On the coast north-west of Kilmalkedar lies the fishing village of Ballydavid, where the traditional curraghs - light but sea-worthy vessels of tarred canvas on a framework of laths - are still made.

At Ballynaveooragh, some distance inland at the foot of Brandon Mountain (second highest in Ireland at 3,127 feet), can be found a large group of beehive huts, several of them double, and two stone ring-forts. The coast at Brandon Head, where Masatiompan (2,461 feet) falls down to the sea, has a series of mighty cliffs. On Brandon Mountain are the remains of St Brandon's Oratory and a number of stone huts.

Direct from Dingle a road runs over the 1,254 feet Connor Pass, through a grandiose landscape of rugged gorges and steep rock faces. At the foot of the pass the road to the left leads to Cloghane and Brandon, the one straight ahead returns to Camp. To the right of this road is Beenoskee (2,713 feet), whilst to the left a long promontory reaches out into the sea. The road continues to Castlegregory, a quiet little resort between Tralee Bay and Lough Gill (see 10 November 1580 in Chapter 3). Back towards Dingle, one crosses a miniature pass between two mountains; and from there to Anscaul, from where another road leads over the mountains to Tralee Bay, on the north side of the Peninsula, by way of the Connor Pass.

At the time of the beginning of the Munster Plantation the Dingle peninsula was again to see some excitement.

Following the defeat of the Spanish Armada in the English Channel during July-August 1588, several Spanish ships managed to escape up around the east coast of Britain, and round the top of Scotland. In September the progress of these 13 or so ships was being reported by English garrisons all down the western coast of Ireland. The crews of many were in a bad way through injury, disease or hunger, with a great number dying daily and having to be thrown overboard. Some of these vessels were to become wrecked, with the crews being either drowned, or dying through their wounds, hunger or thirst, taken prisoner and/or killed.

<u>8 September 1588.</u> Spanish ships arrived in the Sound of Blasgay (Blasquets) off Dingle, with a letter from one of the captains being sent by the Suffrein of Dinglcush (Dominick Ryesse) to Vice-President Thomas Norreys. A Scotchman (*sic*) taken prisoner reported the Spaniards sick,

> destitute of victuals, and in great extremity. (*CSPI 1588-92, Vol. CXXXVI*)

<u>16 September 1588.</u> Sir Henry Wallop wrote from Cork to Lord Burghley, that the Spanish ships which tried to sail from Dingle were turned back by the wind. (*CSPI 1588-92, Vol. CXXXVI*) Offshore big seas which run with a full gale from the north-north-west apparently create long parallel ribbons of foam downwind that stretch for miles.

Eventually three surviving ships neared the Blasket Islands, though they were also to see two others come to grief off Tralee. Sir Edward Denny was the local commander of the area around Tralee in co. Kerry; and it was his wife who after parleying with 25 surrendering survivors of one such unknown-named wreck in the Bay of Tralee - to determine their origin - then proceeded to have them hanged. Another ship came to grief:

> one great hulk of 400 tons, which was so spoiled as she cast towards the shore about 20 leagues from Dingle-i-couch

off Tralee, with the crew suffering a similar fate from the local inhabitants. This was possibly the *Trinidad*.

The great 1,050-ton *San Juan* managed to negotiate the difficult narrow entrance into Blasket Sound, not far from Dingle. For centuries before the reign of Queen Elizabeth, and during it, hundreds of Spanish fishing boats were operating off the Irish coasts, which at that time were greatly productive of fish. There was therefore no shortage of skilled pilots in the Spanish Armada. There was also at this time the 750-ton galleon *San Juan Bautista*, and a 40-ton pinnace. Because of their size they were able to beat off any attack from land, and commenced to take on drinking water. After three days, on the morning of 21 September, a strong westerly gale began to blow huge seas through the anchorage, and the larger *San Juan* began to drift towards the other and eventually bumped against her, causing some damage.

Two more Spanish ships then approached the anchorage, one being the 945-ton 26-guns *Santa Maria de la Rosa*, also known as the *Nuestra Senora de la Rosa*, commanded by Martin Villafranca, the vice-flagship of Miguel Oquendo's 'Armada of Guipuzcoa'. She was signalling obvious signs of distress but managed to anchor. She then started to drift on the ebb tide, whilst sinking at the same time with loss of all life except for the pilot's young son, who drifted ashore to be taken prisoner - and then apparently killed after interrogation. The smaller *San Juan* had started to drift towards this wreck, but managed to heave-to in time. A further derelict then appeared later in the afternoon, another *San Juan*, and continued disintegrating in the storm. She was to eventually join the *Nuestra Senora de la Rosa* at the bottom of the Sound. Both vessels still had all their artillery on board.

The surviving vessels managed later to put out to sea to continue their stormy voyage back to Spain. The shore garrisons had been unable to stop them watering, but had been able to take a few prisoners. Swollen corpses then began to rise from the wrecks at the bottom of the Sound, and drift to shore. The place of their burial was named

Uaig Mhic Ri Na Spáinne, the 'Grave of the Son of the King of Spain', for it was wrongly believed at the time that the Prince of Ascoli had been one of those perishing there.

The following year Sir George Carew, (who had been knighted 1585/6, and appointed Master of the Ordnance 1587/8), went across to Ireland to undertake salvage from the sunken Spanish wrecks, - to recover where possible any money, treasure, and artillery that had not already been taken by the local inhabitants. Apparently the Dingle Peninsula was included in his itinerary.

In 1963 a search began for the wreck of the *Santa Maria* in Blasket Sound, but nothing was found until 1968. It was the following year that its location was confirmed, but not much bodywork or contents were discovered. Fuller details of the Armada wrecks around Ireland may be found in Alexander McKee's *From Merciless Invaders*.

LOCATIONS OF CHAPMAN GRANTS IN MUNSTER

MacCarthy-Morrogh had confirmed that the Champen/Champion lands were situated around Dingle and Smerwick, with a small portion at Ballymacdonell (after which the seignory is named) between Castleisland and Currans in central co. Kerry.

Comparing as far as possible the 1588/9 Fiants with the 1584 Desmond Survey translation in the editions of *The Kerryman* August-October 1927 it is more able to determine the locations, etc. of many of these various grants and leases. Names were not always identifiable, nor the *Survey* 100% complete to be able to locate all lands mentioned. Also to be taken into account is that names were originally in Gaelic, spelt phonetically, mis-heard or mis-read.

According to O'Hart, down to the mid-17th century almost all places in Ireland were known under Irish names, each of which had its own special significance. But in the last clause of the Acts of Settlement and Explanation (1661-1665) it was enacted that the Lord Lieutenant and Council might direct that in all Patents by which Lands were granted in Ireland, only English names of places were to be used. The original Irish name of a place has a relatively clear meaning which often conveys something of its history. But the English rule that placenames were anglicised to suit the English tongue often means that the result is that the name on the map is a mangled version of the real name, and hides its meaning.

Other details are derived from Samuel Lewis's *Topographical Dictionary of Ireland* of the 1840s. References to the King James I 40-year leases of 1606/7 to 'John Champen' (see Chapter 4) are also included here, plus *Census of Ireland 1901*, and King's *County Kerry Past and Present*.

There is one serious question of doubt. One source (Hickson) says that the joint grant to Stone and Champen was for the whole of the barony of Corkaguiny (getting on for 160,000 acres); whereas others say it was for just some 1,434 acres, without specifying whether they were

Irish or English acres. MacCarthy Morrogh has since kindly reiterated his coverage of this point, originally made in his thesis.

As mentioned in the thesis, the area of lands mentioned in the 16th Report (see Chapter 4) was not stated, but they were measured by Jobson in 1586/87 as 1,041 acres (*SP/63/131/59*); or 979 acres (*SP/63/133/96*). Then in 1611 stated as 1,680 acres (PROI *1A/48/64, No. 4*); in 1622 as 1,424 acres (*Journal of the Royal Society of Antiquaries of Ireland, No. 54*, page 138 of 1924). Finally, c.1631 it was 1,434 acres (Chatsworth *Lismore MSS, Boyle patent book*, page 379). MacCarthy Morrogh points out that

> only profitable land was counted; with all the surrounding mountain and scrub the overall acreage was probably double or treble the amount - perhaps 5,000 acres...to estimate the size is to stick to the lower figure but with the proviso that only profitable land was assessed. The whole business of actual, precise acreages is a minefield.

Thus Hickson was incorrect to say that Stone and Champion were awarded the whole barony of Corkaguiny or Ballymacdonnell. It was clearly just the seignory of Ballymacdonnell, of which nobody had much idea of the exact amount of land involved:

> the government assumed a full sized seignory at first, and therefore gaily bestowed '12,000' acres; then decreased this notional amount to '8,000' acres. Finally when Jobson, the surveyor, got around to some precise measurements, the amount turned out to be approximately 1,500 acres.

Adding the individual stated or estimated areas in the relevant *Fiant 5308* joint grants there is around the 1,434 acres assessed. However, whilst this *Fiant* details specific properties and land, it finishes by saying 'and all other lands escheated within the trokahid of Corkoneyny, Kerry.' These 'other lands' may be found in copies of *The Kerryman* of 1927, but generally only those specified in the *Fiants* have been visited by the author as far as practicable.

County KERRY

ACKRIE/ACKRY- 'land and rectory of.' *Fiant 5306* lease. Gaelic: Na hAcral. Grid Ref: Q 000570.

1901: 'Acres- 812 acres 2 rods 35 perches, in parish of Ballinusher, barony of Corkaguiny.' It is considered that it is in fact Ballinvoher parish.

ADDERGEWILL- 'land in.' *Fiant 5306* lease. Gaelic = Eadar Ghabhall (meaning land between two river prongs, being between two tributaries of the Crompaun River which flows eventually into the River Cashen). Present name: Addergown. Grid Ref: Q 845343. Approx. 17 miles north of Tralee.

1901: 'In parish of Rattoo, barony of Clanmaurice.'

AGHAHAMALLY- 'fourth part of rectory of.' *Fiant 5306* lease. It has not been possible to locate this.

ARDCULLEN- 'land in.' *Fiant 5306* lease. Ardcullen = holly hill. About 20 miles north of Tralee. Grid Ref: Q 876367.

1901: 'With Ardcullen Marshes in parish of Rattoo, barony of Clanmaurice.'

Generally flatlands. There is a small private local museum housed in business premises down a short drive, but containing little or nothing of interest to the period under consideration.

BALLENTERMON Ballintermon. Baile an tearmoin = the town of the sanctuary. Grid Ref: Q 607025.

The Kerryman 13 August 1927: 'One other parcel of land called Ballinterymyn, in the parish of Ballynecourty, containing by estimation 80 acres of land, £4.9s.'

1606/7: 'Part of 250 acres lease.'

1901: 'In parish of Ballynacourty, barony of Corkaguiny.'

BALLIBROMAINE- 'land of.' *Fiant 5306* lease. Ballybroman = Boor or rustic baile. Grid Ref: Q 812216

1901: 'Ballybroman, in parish of O'Dorney (q.v.), barony of Clanmaurice. 261 acres 2 rods 16 perches.'

When visited was arable, and cow pasture.

<u>BALLIGAHILL</u>- See McEDMONDS.

<u>BALLIHOA</u> (with LATINIORE *q.v.*)

1606/7 lease: 'Stone house newly built, Latiniore & Ballihoa containing 250 acres of land.' It has not been possible to locate this.

<u>BALLINESITOR and CHURCHTOWNE</u>- *1606/7*: 'Town and lands of 100 acres containing a good house thereon.' It has not been possible to locate these.

<u>BALLY M'DONNELLS</u>- 'the village and butt end of a castle with appurtenances, late of.' *Fiant 5308*. Bally M'Donnells = the townland of Donnell's son..

MacCarthy-Morrogh says this was the small area after which the seignory was named, situated between the seignories of Castleisland owned by Sir William Herbert, and Currans owned by Charles Herbert. Was this the area of dispute between Sir William and Chapman? Herbert arrived at Castleisland 26 April 1587, having been granted 12,000 acres at 4d per acre, as did John Champion [sic] for his.

The Kerryman 17 September 1927: 'The Barony or Canthred of the Troghakede of Enackmy alias Makemy is valued...A castle and village called Ballymacdaniell, late in the possession of M'Daniel, containing 4 carrucates of land filled with some underwood which said lands devolved to the said Earl for default of heirs of the said M'Daniel, before the rebellion, and are valued, per annum, at £13.6s.8d.'

1606/7 lease: 'Part Land of Ballin M^c^Donnell containing 100 acres, with a house built. Lands of Killalownes part of BallinMcDonnell containing 100 acres of land and a smaller tenement built thereupon.'

1901: Ballymacdonnell in parish of Killeentierna, barony of Trughanacmy. 178 acres 0 rods 3 perches. The ruins of the old parish church still remain in the burial ground.

When this location (Grid Ref: Q 965072) was visited in July 2000 there was found a farm called Ballymacdonnell, with an original part of the farmhouse said to be 300 years old. Local historian Michael Culloty says there was never a castle there, only a stone fort of which there are still some remains.

BALLYNECORTY- 'late of Morish m'Shane Hussee land of.' *Fiant 5308.* On south coast of Dingle Peninsula, just west of Anscaul. Grid Ref: Q 585022.

The Kerryman 13 August 1927: 'And so the lands and possessions of the aforesaid Maurice Hussey, who lately was the true ancestor of the rector of Ballinecourty, are valued in toto per annum, in lawful money of England payable annually, at the aforesaid feasts equally, £19 13s 4d.'

The Kerryman 1 October 1927: 'MAURICE McSHANE HUSSEY, ALIAS CALLED "HUSSEY" OF GLAUNGORTENKORRANE REBEL AND DECEASED IN WAR AGAINST THE LADY THE QUEEN AS WELL AT THE TIME OF HIS ENTRANCE INTO REBELLION AS AT THE TIME OF HIS DEATH IN THE SAME. And so the lands [see also Clonduffs and Farren Edyllhe] and possessions of the aforesaid Maurice Hussey, who lately was the true ancestor of the rector of Ballinecourty, are valued in toto per annum, in lawful money of England payable annually, at the aforesaid feasts [Easter and Michaelmas] equally, £19.13s.4d.'

King says that Maurice was the 'Son of Thomas Hussey of Ballynacourty'; and that the Husseys (possibly Anglo-Norman) held Dingle and other castles for the Earl of Desmond, and were confiscated with him in 1583.

1606/7: 'Ballinecourtie, part of 250 acre lease.'

1901: In parish of Ballynacourty, barony of Corkaguiny. 362 acres 2 rods 4 perches.

The rectory is impropriate in the Earl of Cork. There are remains of the ancient church in the burial ground.

Ballynacourty is a half-Irish, half-English name, said to mean 'the town of the judgement seat', recalling the fact that a Seneschal's court once exercised jurisdiction within its area.

According to *The Kerryman* of 22 October 1927, in one of a series of articles 'Antiquities of the Barony of Corkaguiny', the last wolf in Ireland was killed near Ballyduff (north side of Peninsula), at a place now called

'Wolf Step', but no date is given. King however says that 'In 1712, at Maghanaboe [cow's lawn] wolf step, the last of the wolves was killed.' - Grid Ref: Q 565078.

<u>BALLYNEIGHE</u>- 'land of.' *Fiant 5308.* Grid Ref: Q 364037. Gaelic: Baile an Eanaigh. It is believed to have been the following:

The Kerryman 13 August 1927: 'A parcel of land called Ballenea, in the parish of Marynne [Marhin], late in the possession of John M'Ulick, attainted of High Treason, and executed at the City of Limerick, containing by estimation 160 acres of land £4.'

Lewis: 'Maurhin or Marhir. Present name of parish: Marhyn. 5½ miles north-west of Dingle, on south shore of Smerwick Harbour. On the hill of Ballyneanig is a Druidical circle; and a short distance south-east are two large upright stones or gallans. In the vicinity are the remains of a stone cell of great antiquity. Also an old castle built by one of the Desmond family, and afterwards the residence of the Moriarties.'

1606/7: 'Town and lands of Ballyneigh containing 100 acres on which a house built.'

King: 'Ballineanig, castle and church quarters. The town of the aenach or fair.'

MacCarthy-Morrogh says there is a medieval church still *in situ*.

<u>BALLYUSIN alias BALLIUSUR</u>- 'land and rectory of.' *Fiant 5306* lease. Ballyusane is in the parish of Odorney (q.v.). Possibly the Ballysheen at Grid Ref. Q 835244.

<u>BOHER RO/ROE</u>- land and rectory of. *Fiant 5306* lease. Boher = road for cattle. Boherroe = red road. Grid Ref: Q 861225.

1901: Boherroe in parish of Odorney (*q.v.*), near Tralee, barony of Clanmaurice.

When the site was visited in July 2000 what could have been an old cattle road was still in existence, leading down to old farm buildings. Much of the soil and stone in Ireland is of a pink colour, which could easily have been the reason for so naming this location.

BYNNARTER- *1606/7*: Part of 250 acre lease. It has not been possible to identify this location.

CHURCHTOWNE- see BALLINESITOR.

CLONDUFFS (TWO)- 'land of.' *Fiant 5308*. Coumduffe = the black valley. Just north of Anascaul, on the narrow road to Lough an Scail, there are two townlands: one named An Com Dubh Beag (Little Clonduff) at Grid Ref: Q 570037, and another called An Com Dubh Mór (Large Clonduff) at Grid Ref: Q 584040.

The Kerryman 1 October 1927: 'And [Maurice McShane Hussey] was similarly seized of two villages called the Two Clonduffs, parcels of land arable, pasture, feeding, moor, furzes, briars, underwoods, bogs, and other waste which are extended as lying near Lougheskall (at 4d. per acre per annum), at £4.' See also Ballynecourty and Farren Edyllhe.

1606/7: Comeduff part of 250 acre lease.

Land appears to be down to grassland for cattle and silage/hay.

CLONECANROIRKE- 'land and rectory of.' *Fiant 5306* lease. It has not been possible to identify this location.

CLONENYMETAUGHE/CLONENYMENTAUGHE- 'land and rectory of.' *Fiant 5306* lease. In the parish of Odorney (q.v.)., being possibly Cloonametagh at Grid Ref: Q 852219.

COMBALLYHEE- See BALLYHE.

DINGLECUSHE alias DINGLE- According to *King*:

Dingle, a deep dell or little wooded hollow, is the name of a parish in Corcaguiny, and composed of 35 townlands, viz.: Ballyameenboght, Ballybeg, Ballycanneen, Ballyeightragh, Ballyheaboght, Ballymacadoyle, Ballymorereagh, Ballynabooly, Ballingoleen or Burnham, Cappa, Carhoo, Cliddaun, Clossmore, Commons of Dingle, Commons of Milltown, Cullenagh, Dingle, Doonsheane, Emlagh, Farran, Farranflaherty, Farrannakilla, Farranredmond, Glin, Gortanimerisk,

Gortonora, Grove, Killelane, Knockeen, Milltown, Monacappa, Mullenaglemig, Raheenyhooig, Reenbey, Wood,..The Earl of Desmond had a castle in Dingle; it was confiscated in 1585, and the Corporation used the vaults as the town gaol,..The tombstone inscriptions in Dingle include those of Stephen Rice, 1629 [see below],..In 1590 Dingle town had one main street, with gates in times past, and smaller streets on either side, and a castle also; the Earl of Desmond burned the town of Daingean y Cuis, or Castle Cove, Dingle cuishe, or dell cove,..King James granted the house of John Hussey [see below] to the Corporation to be used as a meeting place, and also as a prison or jail [and also a common courthouse, etc.],

Also in King's *Parishes of Kerry*:

This place was anciently called Daingean-ui-Chuis, the stronghold or castle of the O'Cush family, The Earl of Desmond granted the Hussey family a settlement here, After the Desmond forfeitures the district was given to the Earl of Ormonde, who sold it to the Knight of Kerry, After the destruction of the Spanish forces at Smerwick in 1581 many of the English soldiers died from sickness in Dingle, Queen Elizabeth granted £300 to build a wall round the town, In 1600 the Sugan Earl of Desmond, having been refused admittance into the Knight of Kerry's castle, set the town on fire, The town is said to have had three castles, the sites of which are still pointed out,..In 1585 Queen Elizabeth ordered a grant of a charter in incorporation to the town,..The old church of St, James was built by the Spaniards,..In 1605 the town of Dingle consisted of one main street, with gates at either end, and a castle, The houses were built with thick stone walls and narrow windows,..The English sailors who visited Dingle in [c,1589] did not relish the local beer, "We had of them some 10 or 11 Tunnes of beere,.., but it proved like a present purgation to them that tooke it so that we chose rather to drinke water than it,"

Hitchcock quotes further from this interesting contemporary 1589 account.

Hussey had built a castle here, with vaults later used as the town gaol. Several houses were built in the Spanish fashion, with ranges of stone balcony windows. Most of these houses were of stone, with marble door and window frames. This reflected the place being much frequented by ships from Spain, who traded with the inhabitants, and came to fish on the coast. On one house was an inscription, signifying that it was built by one by the name of Rice in 1563. Rice (Rees, Rhys, Price) was a prominent Welsh/Norman family, as well as Hussey. Where the catholic Presbytery now stands on Main Street was a Rice house, 'the highest house on the hill'. And on a stone, beneath two roses, was carved "At the Rose is the Best Wine". Many houses had dates on them from Queen Elizabeth's time, and even earlier.

Dingle was occupied by a French force during the Rebellion of James Fitzmaurice Fitz Gerald in 1570; and in 1579 he landed Spanish ships in the port, and subsequently burned the town. He was one of the many to be killed at Smerwick in 1580. Dingle was besieged and burnt again during this turbulent period, and seems to have been largely abandoned, so that it became necessary to devise ways by which fishermen and merchants could be encouraged to return to the town. Hence the actions of Elizabeth and James I. According to Hitchcock, in 1585 Elizabeth signed a warrant for the grant of a Charter for Dingle to become a borough, plus £300 for walling the new borough. But in the event the walling was done on a piecemeal basis, and the Charter was not actually granted until 1608 by James I.

In Green Street, near its junction with Main Street, there is a stone marked '1586' on the wall of a shop, probably from a house built following the destruction of the town after the Desmond wars. Two other houses further down Green Street have other surviving small decorated panels, said to have come from houses of Spanish merchants in the town, with tradition saying that they indicated the nature of the business carried on.

Dingle was burned again in 1600 by the súgán Earl of Desmond. (Súgán Earl = Earl of Straw)

As late as 1830 the road between Tralee and Dingle was very bad, and the post was exchanged between a runner from each town at the half-way mark.

The *Fiant 5308* joint-grant properties in Dingle town to Stone and Champen were:

'the park'-

The Kerryman 13 August 1927: 'A parcel of land adjacent to the said [ruinous chief] mansion [late in tenure of Edmond Russel in the town of Dinglecushe] called the Park formerly a wood, containing 35 acres of land in the tenure of the said Edmond Russel, [13s4d].'

Subsequent to this the area was called 'Orchard', said to be a corruption of 'Archard', being the place where archery was practised in byegone days. In July 2000 it is now the 'Town Park', with at one end part of the Elizabeth/James I town wall.

'a mill'-

The Kerryman 13 August 1927: 'And also a water mill in Dingle aforesaid, together with a house and garden and four acres of arable land adjacent to the same, £2 13s 4.'

This was situated just to the west of Dingle, at Milltown, after the bridge. Nothing is visible now except the silting-up river, which was once said to be a 'race'.

'house within the town, sometime in tenure of David Brenaghes, 6s 8d a year'-

The Kerryman 13 August 1927: 'One tenement, with the appurtenances, lying in the town of Dingle formerly the property of David Brenoghes, which came to the aforesaid late Earl by Escheat, worth per annum 6s. 8d.'

'house with appurtenances called Ballibradoughe, 13s4d a year'-

The Kerryman 13 August 1927: 'Another tenement, with appurtenances, escheated to the aforesaid Earl, lying in the said town of Dingle, called Ballybradagh 13s. 4d.'

'house between lands of Stephen Rice on the north & east, and of Thomas M'Gerrot on the south, 6s 8d a year'-)

The Kerryman 13 August 1927: 'Another tenement similarly

escheated to the aforesaid late Earl, in Dingle aforesaid, between the lands of Stephen Rice on the North and East, and the lands of Thomas M'Garrett on the South side, 6s 8d.'

King said there was a tombstone of a Stephen Rice marked 'MDCXXII' in Dingle churchyard

'<u>house and garden late of David duffe Gerrald</u>, 3s4d a year'–)

The Kerryman 1 October 1927: 'DAVID DUFF GERALD, A REBEL, WHO DIED IN WAR AGAINST THE QUEEN, AT THE TIME OF HIS ENTRANCE INTO REBELLION AS AT THE TIME OF HIS DEATH IN REBELLION. Was seized in his demesne as of fee, of and in one tenement in Dinglecush with a garden and its appurtenances, at present broken and wasted, of which a certain Thomas Moore, claims to have a mortgage for a sum of 15s. sterling. And they are valued per annum in lawful money of England, payable at the aforesaid feasts [Easter and Michaelmas] equally at 3s 4d.'

The many gifted David Duffe Fitz Gerald (usually called David Duffe) was born in Kerry, and was to be killed in June 1581 fighting on Desmond's side. His Dingle property was thus confiscated.

'<u>house with land late of John Hussie</u>, slain in rebellion, 10s a year.'–

The Kerryman 1 October 1927: 'JOHN HUSSEY, ALIAS JAMES HUSSEY, LATE OF DINGLECUSH SLAIN IN REBELLION AGAINST THE QUEEN AT THE TIME OF HIS ENTRANCE INTO REBELLION, AS WELL AT THE TIME OF HIS DEATH IN REBELLION. Was seized in his demesne, as of fee of in a tenement in the town of Dingle aforesaid with the appurtenances, and 4 acres of land in the fields there, valued per annum by the aforesaid Commissioners, in lawful money of England, to be paid at the aforementioned festivals of Easter and Michaelmas, by equal portions, 10s.'

This was the market house given by charter by Elizabethg/James I. In July 2000 the site was occupied by Fitzgerald's store on the south side of Main Street, near its junction with Green Street, with a plaque recording the above association. The locations of none of the other houses have been possible.

'burgage and garden late of James Russell, 15s a year.'-

The Kerryman 8 October 1927: 'A tenement or burgage with a garden there, and its appurtenances, lately the property of James Russel, deceased, in rebellion, which was mortgaged to Richard Traunt, a burgess there (possibly Anglo-Norman), for £15, as is reported value, per annum money, 15s.'

Amongst the 'Bills of Complaint' dated 3 September 1588 (*CSPI 1588-92 Vol. CXXXVI*) was one by:

Richard Trant of Dangley [Dingle], co. Kerry claims a stone house and garden in Dangley against one Thomas Hayford, who claims the same to the use of Her Majesty. Claim dismissed.

'two burgages with a garden late of Dominick Fitz Morishe, 10s a year.-)

The Kerryman 8 October 1927: 'Two burgages, with a garden in the said Burgh of Dingle, lately the property of Dominic Fitz-Morris, a rebel, and fugitive to Spain; valued per annum (besides 3s. 4d, free rent due to James Traunt), 10s.' Fitz Maurice was possibly another Anglo-Norman.

'a tenement, late of Thomas fitz William ne Boy, 5s a year.'-

The Kerryman 8 October 1927: 'And a tenement or messuage, with the appurtenances in the said Town of Dingle, lately the property of Thomas Fitz-William Bowy, attained, now almost wasted; worth per annum, in similar money, 5s.'

DOURKYNE- 'land of.' *Fiant 5308*. Grid Ref: Q 320005. Donkyne = Dunquin, at western end of Dingle peninsula.

The Kerryman 13 August 1927: 'A parcel of land called Downekyne in the parish of Downekyne, containing by estimation 200 acres. £4.'

1606/7: 'Town & lands of Downkyne, 100 acres, and a small tenement built thereupon.'

According to Lewis: 'Dunmore Head is the most westerly point of Ireland. On the rocky coast of this parish are often found the beautiful crystals called Kerry stones. The ruins of the church still remains in the burial-ground, where the [alleged] Prince of Ascule was interred after the wreck here of part of the Spanish Armada.

According to King:

...the Blasquet islands [just off the end of the Dingle peninsula], seized by the Fitz Geralds, were held by the Ferriter family until 1586, when they were confiscated to Geo. Stone and Con Chapman, who sold them to Sir Richard Boyle.

This must be the Cornelius Chapman mentioned under 1586 in Chapter 4. The Blaskets had a dual economy of farming and fishing. Farming was based on medieval communal tillage, with use of horse-drawn ploughs. Sheep were kept for all purposes, i.e. meat, wool and skins. Oats were the main cereal, with diet also of fish, rabbit, and edible seaweed, and later potatoes. Turf and furze were used for fuel. Crabs and lobsters were exported, though the Islands could be cut-off for weeks by storms. Buildings were built of stone. Hitchcock wrote in 1852 that the Blaskets were 'celebrated for fattening sheep, and the flavour of the mutton they produce is excellent.'

DROMYCOMYGENYN- 'land and rectory of.' *Fiant 5306* lease. Dromycounygengn was in the parish of Odorney (*q.v.*). It has not been possible to trace this location.

FARREN EDYLLHE near Lescache- 'land of.' *Fiant 5308.* Or Farrenedell.

The Kerryman 1 October 1927 (*q.v.* Ballyhe above): 'Was seized in his [Maurice McShane Hussey] demesne as of fee of and in six quarters and 20 acres of arable land, pasture, moor, furzes, briars, underwoods, and other wastes, called Farren Edille (sic), lying nigh unto Lougheskall, which are extended by the aforesaid Commissioners per annum, in lawful money of English, at the rate of £2 13s

4d. per quarter, at £16 13s 4d.' (See also BALLINECOURTY and CLONDUFFS)

Mary Hickson had no knowledge of this location, and neither has the author, though the names of several townlands begin with 'Farren'.

<u>GALLIE</u>- 'half the rectory of, with the other half belonging to the vicar there.' *Fiant 5306*. Present name: Galey, in Listowel Rural District.

Lewis: A parish in the barony of Iraghticonnor, 8½ miles south-west of Tarbert, 10 miles north-east of Tralee, on the River Galey. 12,605 statute acres, of which nearly $^2/_5$ was bog before draining started.

King: 'In 1302 Galy parish was valued for tithes at 26s 8d...Church in ruins [1756]'

<u>GLANGERTARKARRANE</u>- 'late of Morish m'Shane Hussee - land of.' *Fiant 5306*. Or Glangortennarran. Gortcurrauin - The reaping-hook field. It has not been possible to trace this location. See also Ballynecourty, Clonduffs, and Farren Edyllhe.

The Kerryman 1 October 1927: 'MAURICE McSHANE HUSSEY, ALIAS CALLED "HUSSEY" OF GLAUNGORTENKORRANE...'

<u>KILLALOWNES</u>- See BALLY M'DONNELLS.

<u>KILLGANE</u>- Killegane = the church of the hollow. Is a baile or townland in Castleisland parish.

1606/7: 'Part of a 250 acre lease.'

<u>LACKIMORE</u>- 'land and rectory of.' *Fiant 5306* lease. In parish of Odorney (*q.v.*). Lacka More, just south of Abbeydorney. Grid Ref: Q 857215.

<u>LACKYBEGE/LACKIBEGE</u>- 'land and rectory of.' *Fiant 5306* lease. In parish of Odorney (q.v.). Lacka Beg, just south of Abbeydorney. Grid Ref: Q 848208

<u>LATTINIORE</u> with BALLIHOA-

1606/7 lease: 'Stone house newly built, Latiniore &

Ballihoa containing 250 acres.' Possibly:

The Kerryman 13 August 1927: 'A parcel lying in the parishes of Marynne and Kilmoylekeyther called Latymore containing 200 acres of land, Irish measure. £6.13s.4d.'

LETRYNNE- See McEDMONDS.

LISELTIN- 'half the rectory of, with other half belonging to the vicar there.' *Fiant 5306* lease. (Grid Ref: Q 929395)

1901: 'Lisselton, near Listowel in the barony of Iraghticonnor.'

Smith: 'Church in repair.' Has since been built on by another.

King: 'In 1302 Liseltyn was valued at 26s 8d for tithes.'

MALLAHIFFE- 'rectory of.' *Fiant 5306*. Present name: Molahiffe. Halfway between Killarney and Tralee. Grid Ref: Q 915043

Smith: 'Vicarial. Church in ruins.' Proxy 5s fee.

Lewis: 'In the barony of Magonihy. 4½ miles north-east from Milltown. The parish extends to the summit of Slieve Meesh on the north, and comprises 9,808 statute acres. The rectory is impropriate, but the amount not given. The ruins of the old church still remain, as are those of three castles.' (Seignory itself was granted to Sir Valentine Browne.) Another report says there was very little left in 1841.

King: 'Magofflahith in 1302 was valued at 13s 4d for tithes.'

McEDMONDS- 'lands of.' *Fiant 5308*. On Brandon Bay. Grid Ref: Q 591123

The Kerryman 8 October 1927: 'Nicholas Gerald (sic) Alias M'Edmond. The town and lands of Strabbally.'

Lewis: Stradbally is a parish in the barony of Corkaguiney, 10 miles N.E. of Dingle, containing 1202 inhabitants, of whom 336 are in the village. The soil is in general light, and there are some patches of bog. The village of Stradbally comprises 53 houses, mostly thatched. The rectory is impropriate in the Earl of Cork, and the vicarial tithe-rent charge is £138.15s. In the cemetery adjoining the village are the ruins of the church.

1606/7 lease: 'Town and lands of Balligahill & Letrynne being of the Mc Edmondes land contg 400 acres of land, with dwelling house erected upon Balligahill.'

1901: 'Stradbally Mountain township 596 acres 0 rods 33 perches.'

King: '...compromises 15 bailes, viz:- Ardbeg, Barrack, Cappateige, Cutteen, Fahamore, Farrandalogue, Farrannakilla, Farrantoolen, Garrywilliam, Glennahoo, Gowlane, Knockacurrane, Scraggane, Stradbally mountain, Teerbrin. In 1302 Ardbaly was valued at 20s. for tithes, so Strad Baile is a modern name for the old church in the cemetery.'

<u>MENARDE</u> late of Shane m'Edmond M'Ullicke- 'land of.' *Fiant 5308.*

1606/7: 'Manegarand- Part of 250 acre lease.'

1901: 'Minard parish consists of West Minard 512 acres 2 rods 16 perches, and East Minard 146 acres 3 rods 31 perches.'

King: 'Shane of Ardnagragh was a descendant of Thomas Fitzgerald, Baron of the Island of Kerry c.1300, as was Maurice Duffe and Edward of Corcaguiney...Mynard church in 1302 was valued at 5s for tithes for the vicar.'

This seems to be MINARD, five miles along the coast east of Dingle. Grid Ref: V 555992. It has the remains of a castle, a stronghold of the FitzGerald Knights of Kerry, typical of the tower houses that were built between 1440 and 1600 as residences and fortresses of the nobility. Particularly well-sited above the cove by a bridge over a stream, it was the last of the FitzGerald castles to be built on the peninsula, and probably dates to the late 16th century. Three storey survive, but a fourth probably existed above. The 1st and 2nd were vaulted, but the vaults collapsed in the Cromwellian bombardment and explosions of 1650. On the spur to the east was a pre-Norman ring-fort. 200 yards west is the well of St. John the Baptist, now dressed with a curved stone surround and a simple cross cut into a small stone. On the hill above the well there are a few remains of the early church of

St. Mary, giving the area the name of Kilmurry from the Gaelic form Cill Mhuire. The church's remains dimensions are 40 feet x 20 feet, with a wall 3-5 feet high enclosed by an old stone ditch of an oblong 88 feet x 66 feet.

ODORNEY- 'Site of the abbey of Odorney alias our lady abbey of Kyryleison, and rectory of.' *Fiant 5306* lease. Grid Ref: Q 851236

Lewis: 'The parish/village of Odorney/Abbeydorney is in the barony of Clanmaurice, seven miles N. by E. from Tralee. It takes its name from the ancient abbey of 'Kyrie Eleison' or 'O'Dorney', an abbey under the invocation of the Virgin Mary was founded in 1154, for Cistercian monks. Its possessions, at one time very extensive, were at the Dissolution granted by Henry VIII to Edmond, Lord of Kerry, created Baron O'Dorney in 1537. In 1596 the abbey was given by Queen Elizabeth to the Provost and Fellows of Trinity College, Dublin; and in 1603 the rectory (amount not known) of O'Dorney was granted by the queen to William Taaffe, Esq. The ruins of the ancient abbey church are situated just to the north of the village of Abbey-Dorney, but retain few vestiges of its original character.

1606/7: Leased of James I 'late abbey of Oderney, alias Ladies Abbey, of Keriolezen.'

King: 'Mainister o dTorna, abbey Odorney...In 1302 the church of the Monks was valued at 13s 4d for tithes, and the revenue of the house of Kiriel of the order of Cistercians at 7s 4d [or 73s 4d]...In 1603 the late abbey of Odorney, called Our Lady's Abbaye de Kerielizon, contained 1 Church, 2 churchyards, 2 acres arable, 1 water mill, and 170 acres in the parish; demised to John Zouche, later to John Champen, then to Wm. Taaffe, and finally to Crosbie family. The abbey lands included 60 acres in Cloghean, Royrke, Dromycounygenyn, Moneacrie, and Ballyusane; 80 acres in Lackimore, Lackibegg, and Clonenymeateagh; 30 acres in Ballybromaine. The abbey ruins are now in need of attention; after many wars since 1154.'

The remains date largely from the 14th century. Stones from the abbey said to have been taken to built crypts on site, and another Catholic church off site. Much of the ground within the ruins has been built up with continual burials; and whilst most of the bones excavated when digging fresh graves are interred with the subsequent coffin, some such bones remain scattered about.

RATHETOWE alias ARRAGENSIS- 'site of the abbey, order of S. Augustin.' *Fiant 5306* lease. Present name: Rattoo, from Ráth Tuaidh (northern ring fort). Some 17 miles north of Tralee. Grid Ref: Q 881336.

Lewis: 'Rattoo, a parish seven miles W. by S. of Listowel. In ancient writings this place is called "Rathtoy". An abbey of Canons Regular of St. Augustine (originally a commandery belonging to the Knights Hospitallers) was founded here in the reign of King John [1199-1216]. It was subsequently occupied by Aroasian Canons, and dedicated to St. Peter and St. Paul; the abbot was a lord of parliament. In 1600 the buildings were fortified by the Irish, but were burned on the approach of Sir Charles Wilmot's forces. The remains of the abbey still exist, with the nearby lofty round tower.'

1606/7: 'Leased of James I.'

King: 'In 1302 the revenue of the house de Rathnoyd of the order of St Augustine was valued at 46s for tithes...In 1573-6, on the dissolution of the monasteries, the Earl of Desmond had a lease of Odorney, Rathtowe, and other abbeys in Munster; when the Earl was proclaimed in 1579, Capt. John Zouche got the leases; and John Champen in 1588; Geo. Isham in 1596...'

Abbey was founded in 1200 as a Hospital, ascribed to the early Kerry saint Lughach, and later became a monastery of Canons Regular of St. Augustine, i.e. priests living in community according to a monastic rule.

The Abbey is said to have been 15th century. The small ruinous church in the nearby graveyard was built probably by the Augustinians in the 15th century, though stones from the earlier church are built into its walls. The Round Tower just outside the graveyard is very well preserved. The land round about is now mostly pasture and arable.

<u>TIRRILASIGHAGHIE</u>- 'land in.' *Fiant 5306* lease. Present name: Tursillagh, also Tor Saileach = sallow (willow) tower. Grid Ref: Q 944150.

Lewis: 'In parish of Ballymacelligott, in the barony of Trughenackmy, 4¾ miles south-east of Tralee. 14,018 statute acres, of which about 2,300 acres are bog and coarse mountain pasture, from which an abundance of limestone and turf might easily be reclaimed. In the northern part of the parish is a romantic glen, called 'Gloun-na-geentha' or Glanageenty, memorable as the scene of the discovery and death in 1583 of then great Earl of Desmond by Kelly, an Irish soldier; his head was sent to London and ordered by Queen Elizabeth to be fixed on London bridge, and his body, after being concealed for some weeks, was interred at Ardnagrath, in a small chapel which still bears his name. The glen forms part of the estate of the Blennerhassett family (another related to Ralegh) owned since the Plantation, and has now been planted. There are remains of forts and a castle in the parish.'

-----oOo-----

County CORK

<u>BALLIAMAINE</u>- 'tithes of the rectory of.' *Fiant 5306* lease. It has not been able to trace this location.

<u>BALLIMANTER</u>- 'tithes of the rectory of.' *Fiant 5306*.
1606/7: Leased of James I the rectory of Ballinter.
It has not been possible to trace this location.

<u>CASTELLAUGHAN alias CASTELLIAN</u>- 'site of the house of friars, with appurtenances.' *Fiant 5307* lease. Now called Castlelyons, some 25 miles N.E. of the city of Cork. At one end of the village main street is a ruined castle, whilst at the other end are the ruins of the friary.

Harbison says it was founded in 1307, by John de Barry for the Carmelite Friars, dedicated to the Blessed Virgin Mary. The present ruins probably date from the 15th century. Ownership came to the Earl of Cork. 'The south wall of the church fell in 1871.'

A detailed description of the ruins may be found in Power's *Archaeological Inventory of County Cork.* In August 2000 it was intended to hold the first Mass here since 1541.

<u>CASTRACAR</u>- 'tithes of the rectory of.' *Fiant 5306* lease. It has not been possible to trace this location; though it may possibly be Castrochore some 15 miles east of Cork city.

<u>CORBO</u>- 'tithes of the rectory of.' *Fiant 5306* lease. It has not been possible to trace this location.

<u>CORK</u>- 'chapel and tithes of St. Nicholas, in the suburbs of Cork. *Fiant 5306* lease.

Lewis: '...the tithes of St Nicholas, and houses producing £5.18s per annum...in the southern part of the city.'

The original church was built before 1186. It was in ruins by 1639, and rebuilt 1720. The present church was built 1849/50.

<u>ITESBACKE</u>- 'tithes of the rectory of.' *Fiant 5306* lease.

1606/7: Leased of James I as Esibacke.

It has not been possible to trace this location.

<u>KINSALE</u>- 'site of the house of friars of the B.V.M., with appurtenances.' *Fiant 5307* lease. 15 miles due south of Cork.

Lewis: 'An abbey of Carmelite Friars, founded and dedicated in 1334 to the Blessed Virgin Mary, but there are no remains. There is a small chapel belonging to the Carmelite friary...'

In 1541 there was reported in existence a 'church with belfry, cloister, hall and other buildings.' It was extensively damaged in 1601 during the siege of Kinsale. What little remains there are of some abbey walls may be found in the centre of the graveyard in Abbey Street. A holy well cut into rockface, also dedicated to St. Mary and which possibly supplied water to the friary, is situated up a short narrow gravel path between two houses just around the corner and up the hill from Abbey Street.

<u>TIMOLAGE or TIMOLEAGUE</u>- 'site of friars house, and appurtenances.' *Fiant 5307* lease.

Lewis: 'Timoleague is a small town 22½ miles S.W. of Cork. Grid Ref: W 4743) It is also called 'Ty-Mologa', signifying the "house of St. Mologa", to whom the Franciscan abbey founded here (either in 1240 or c.1312) was dedicated. The buildings of the abbey, are nearly entire, except the roof, surrounding three sides of a court 60 yards square. On the east is the church. During the reign of [Catholic] Mary [1553-1558] the monks re-took possession of this abbey; and in 1603 [on death of Protestant Elizabeth and accession of Catholic James] the Roman Catholics again occupied it, and completely repaired it in every part.

According to Harbison it was possibly founded either in 1240 or during the period 1327-1377, for the Friars of the Strict Observance of St. Francis. The buildings date from various periods. The original church was probably much shorter than the present one, being possibly lengthened when the tower was added c.1500. Either during the 1598 Rebellion, or in 1612, English soldiers ransacked the friary and smashed beautiful stained glass, burned pictures, and broke statues.

It is attractively sited on a peninsula in Courtmacsherry Bay. Its plan is irregular, as a result of the shape of the peninsula. The buildings were mostly plainly finished. There is a large walled courtyard to the west, a bell-tower, and dormitory. Only a small portion of the cloister remains, but the other buildings are intact.

In the booklet produced by the Timoleague Community Association is the following: 'It was about this time [c.1590] that lease of the friary was acquired by two strangers - Thomas Wyse, and Thomas Chapman. These gentlemen were only interested in what money they could make from the sale and demolition of the Friary. Bishop Lyon, the Protestant Bishop of Ross, bought the mill in 1590 and had it removed to his own neighbourhood. No sooner had he erected it than it was swept away by a flood - the misfortune being attributed by many of the indignation of Heaven. In 1596 an Anglican Minister named Hammer took away some timber and oak wainscotting from cells of the monastery. His work, likewise, suffered a similar curse, for after putting out to sea with his freight a storm sprung up sending the ship, its cargo, and all aboard to the bottom of the ocean.' This reference to a supposed Thomas Chapman is being investigated. With the accession of James I in 1603, the monks emerged from hiding and renovated the friary.

The first picture of the abbey ruins appears to have been c.1780, and also showing ruins of a castle built in 1302, but now gone.

------oOO------

County GALWAY

KILMURRY in Two M'Walter- 'the chapel of in barony of Bealeamo, with land in.' *Fiant 5306* lease. Kilmurry = Church of St. Mary.

1606/7: Leased from James I.

The church was shown as in ruins on 1840 maps. It is approached by taking the N83 road north from Tuam, then just before Browngrove there is a narrow road on the eastern side, marked at the junction with a large stone inscribed CARRATENLIN. Follow this road for almost six miles, and just past what looks to be a prefabricated bungalow the site is in the middle of a grass field on the right. There is a clear outline of the church some 66 feet x 22 feet, with vestiges of wall, particularly at the west end. There is rubble inside, and scattered stones outside.

LISMOHEGE- 'with land in.' *Fiant 5306* lease. It has not been possible to trace this location.

------oOo------

County ROSCOMMON

MONASTERIE EVAN alias KENNETT- 'parcel of land called...lying by the town of Higgens in the barony of Roscoman.' *Fiant 5306* lease.

1606/7: 'Leased of James I.'

According to information received from County Roscommon Heritage & Genealogy Company this may be one of two similarly named locations. These are in the Roman Catholic parish of Ballaghderreen in the north-west of the county, covering parts of counties Roscommon, Sligo, and Mayo. It could be the townland of MONASTERREDEN in the barony of Coolavin, having a long narrow shape, but of unknown dimensions. The other much smaller area is named Annaghbeg Monasterredan. Both are actually over the border in co. Sligo. They have not been visited by the author.

THE MUNSTER REBELLION OF 1598

18 April 1589 The muster roll of Sir Christopher Hatton, Lord Chancellor of England, was delivered by a William Chapman who was recorded as being a vice-constable of Dungarvan Castle. (*CSPI 1588-92, Vol. CXLIII*)

Was this William the brother of John Chapman? Dungarvan is a sea-port in co. Waterford, 22 miles south-west of the town of Waterford. The castle was erected for the town's defence by King John. In the reign of Edward VI (1547-1553) Robert St.Leger, brother to the Lord-Deputy St.Leger (a family related to Ralegh and thus to the Champernownes) was confirmed in the government of the castle, to which he had been appointed in the preceding reign of Henry VIII. Other constables for the crown were subsequently appointed with extensive powers. The castle was later to be vested in the Earl of Cork and his descendants. Though Lewis mentions in 1846:

some interesting REMAINS of the ancient castle,..a massive keep in a quadrilateral area, surrounded with a wall defended by a circular tower at each angle, and formerly mounted with cannon; the entrance is by a narrow passage under a tower gateway, flanked by circular bastions,

By 1970 the remains had been incorporated in the military barracks.

[12 May] 1589 Sir Edward Denny undertook to people a 6,000 acres seignory at Tralee, co. Kerry. Copyholders included a Walter Chapman. (*CSPI 1588-92* and *Carew Mss 169*)

21 August 1589. List of the officers and men who were shipped for the Low Countries this day included Captain Champernon's 65 in the ship *Roger and Catherine* of Newcastle. (*CSP Domestic 1580-1625 Addenda, Vol. XXXI*) It is not known which Champernowne this was.

13 September 1589 Sir William Herbert, the Kerry undertaker, from his house at Tintarne, (Tinterne in Devon), wrote in a 3-page self-interested letter to Lord

Burghley, in which there is about the only written reference directly linking Champion/Chapman with Ralegh:

...Mr Stone, one of Her Majesty's footmen, and Champion, a man of Sir Walter Rawley's, are unable through insufficient means to inhabit the lands they have undertaken in Kerry...the one of them worth little, the other worth nothing, neither of them able to perform what they have undertaken. These 8,000 acres might be given to Winston [cousin, who desires to become an undertaker]. (*CSPI 1588-92, Vol. CXLVI; SP/63/146/41*)

<u>20 May 1590.</u>:

The great necessity of the soldiers who want money. (*CSPI 1588-92, Vol. CLII*)

<u>June 1590.</u> Some of the Queen's ships were off Dingle Cush and Smerwick. (*CSPI 1588-92, CLIII*)

When Ralegh and Grenville went from Munster, the two most forward spirits were withdrawn from the hopeful plantation. The rest were nothing like so active. A commission of 1592 found that of 58 undertakers only 13 were resident, and that there were only 245 English families settled on the land. By 1592 Denny's arrears for chief rents were enormous. The country was far too poor and depopulated to answer these rents.

In 1592 there was a commission to settle disputes. There were 30 cases in Kerry (12 won and 14 lost). Champion was subject to suits, though he may also have been a plaintiff. Cases were brought by local inhabitants as well as settlers. So much land had to be eventually returned by undertakers to local inhabitants (including in Kerry) that rents were accordingly much reduced.

<u>December 1592</u> In the *CSPI*:

Kerry. John Champion hath of rentable lands the number of 1,434 acres; rent from Michaelmas, 1591 - £11.9s.0d, and from Michaelmas 1594 - £23.18s.0d yearly for ever.

1595 Champion was Sheriff of co. Kerry. During the year Hugh O'Neill, afterwards Earl of Tyrone, broke out into open rebellion, though not yet to any large scale extent. This was brought about partly by the measures taken to repress Catholic worship.

1596 Thomas Champion listed as High Sheriff of County Kerry, possibly until 1607. (From a MS 'List of High Sheriffs of Irish Counties', published in Hickson's *Old Kerry Records, 2nd Series*, 1874.

6 February 1596 George Stone applies to make glass in Ireland. The manufacture and exporting of glass was one of the signs of a changing economic future.

13 August 1596 From Dinglecush, John Champion wrote a letter to Thomas Spring:

> The previous afternoon a ship of three or four score tons entered the [Bay of] Smerwick. Above four score men were seen on board. The ship, which was of a great length and of a Spanish build, had gone northwards towards Galway. In all likelihood they are Spaniards.

Three more ships were reported by other observers.

18 July 1597:

> 6. Another practice [of wrongs to be righted in Munster against Her Majesty] is used to abate the revenue, when such as possess Her Majesty's lands can buy the lands to themselves, at a more inferior rate, of persons whom they suborn to pretend title to the lands. This is a usual practice in Munster, practised lately against George Stone, one of Her Majesty's footmen, by Champion, his tenant, who suborned one to make claim to the best part of that land; and having compounded with him for little or nothing beforehand, did afterwards suffer him, with whom he compounded, to recover that parcel from Her Majesty.

These practices may have included Stone's lands since he now disappears from these records, with there being later allegations that Champion was an accomplice to resumption which removed Stone. Champion was accused of conspiring with fellow settlers to find lands unjustly; he was censured, but the finding overruled. This accusation included co-operation with Boyle in passing grants of concealments in the late 1590s. (*CSPI 1596-97*, pages 94 & 346; *SP/63/168/10·1.*)

Presumably this is partly reference *PROI, IA/48/89, No. 14* subsequently re-numbered at the National Archives, but not found when visited in September 1999

Grants upon which patents were passed were all managed by old associates of Richard Boyle. Through them Boyle purchased a part of the grants they managed, with cash payments changing hands. One such patent was passed by Boyle to John Champen, being managed by Patrick Crosby, a bitter enemy of Boyle, and a man of influence in Dublin (who was probably granted the lands of Tarbert in 1607), in conjunction with Morrice Stacke who was an old intimate and ally of Boyle in Kerry. Stacke (or Stack) was possibly from an Anglo-Norman family in Ireland; and Carew was to write of him in 1596: "Maurice Stack and his brother may be trusted." Boyle was witness when Stacke and Champen closed their accounts on 9 March 1600. In the document illustrated (*Lismore Mss*, Vol. 1, no. 39, at Chatsworth House), John Champen's name appears in the top two lines, and Champen's and Boyle's signatures can clearly be seen at the bottom. It was not until 18 June 1604 that Boyle released his right in the land passed on Champen's patent. This grant possessed many livings, impropriate and presentative, supposedly appertaining to Any. Among them were the parsonages of Kynard and Ballinecourty, and the vicarage of Mynard.

It has been seen that the settlers did not come in sufficient numbers; and after the usual fighting and bloodshed, the general result of this Plantation was to displace nearly half the native gentry, and to substitute English proprietors: whilst the majority of the people remained undisturbed. And instead of letting the lands to English tenants, building up a yeomanry as was the intention, and transplanting the strength and solidity of the English society, they were being let to the native Irish. This was to account for the escalation of the troubles which had started in 1595.

Matters really came to a head in October 1598 when there was a countrywide Rebellion by the Irish, plus a great number of degenerate and rebellious English, again with Spanish assistance. The English were to have initial setbacks when the Munster plantattion was attacked by the súgán earl of Desmond.

Many undertakers were no longer in residence on their seignories, or even in Ireland. The undertakers who had stayed in residence were generally servitors and lesser undertakers - many being unfortunate younger sons of families. They had not had estates in England to sell or mortgage to finance their seignories or plantation land, which is why they were found to be soldiering in Ireland in the first place. Champion was said to be still in residence at the time of the Munster rising in October 1598.

Edmund Spenser was also to bewail the lot of the English in this rebellion. He and Ralegh had been neighbours in co. Cork, and Ralegh had visited the other. In 1598 Spenser was appointed Sheriff of Cork, although of failing health. When the rebellion started in the October, he had seemingly been taken unawares. His castle of Doneraile at Kilcolman was burnt over his head, with the possible loss of one of his young children. He then fled to Cork city with his wife and remaining family. In December he was sent by Sir Thomas Norris to London, to advise the government of the situation. But the strain of all the anxieties and his poor health led go his death in January 1599, in an inn or lodgings in Westminster. Sir William St.Leger later purchased the Doneraile estate from the son of the poet, and when lord President of Munster in the reign of Charles I, he held his court here. No remains of the castle now exist.

Sometime in <u>1598</u> it was noted (*CSPI 1598-99*, page 325):

Generally, all the English in Kerry ran away, when there was no rebel within forty miles of them, Castlemayne was long defended by the ward without any means, but their own shifts...

There was no mention of Champion in this particular record, but MacCarthy-Morrogh thinks he was probably involved in the defence of Castlemaine against the rebels.

Richard Boyle escaped to London from this Munster rebellion, for which his enemies held him partly responsible. According to Ranger, aggrieved landowners, established officials whho resented the rise of pushing young men, disinterested royal servants who realised the extent of Boyle's abuse of his office, rivals of Boyle's patron, secretary Fenton, combined to attack Boyle and to protect Burghley against him and his allies. Here he was arrested on the orders of Burghley's son, Robert Cecil, as an obvious scapegoat for a disastrous Irish policy, but the case against him was to be suppressed for expediency's sake for the future of Munster.

Fynes Moryson was later to record in his *Itinerary*:

Many of the Munster men now first about October, 1598, broke into rebellion, and joined themselves with Tyrone's forces, spoiled the country, burnt the villages, and pulled down the houses and castles of the English, against whom (especially the female sex) they committed all abominable outrages...The Munster rebellion broke out like a lightning, for in one month's space almost all the Irish were in rebellious arms, and the English were murdered, or stripped and banished...And to speak the truth, Munster undertakers...., were in great part cause of this defection, and of their own fatal miseries. For whereas they should have built castles and brought over colonies of English, and have admitted no Irish tenant, but only English, these and like covenants were in no part performed by them. Of whom the men of best quality never came over, but made profit of the land; others brought no more English than their own families, and all entertained Irish servants and tenants, which were now the first to betray them. If the covenants had been kept by them, they of themselves might have made 2,000 able men, whereas the Lord President could not find above 200 of English birth among them, when the rebels first entered the Province. Neither did these gentle undertakers make any resistance to the rebels, but left their dwellings and fled to walled towns; yea, when there was such danger in flight, as greater could not have been in defending their own, whereof many of them had woeful experience, being surprised with their wives and children in flight.

26 October 1598. In an Information of William Saxey, Chief Justice of Munster, to Sir Robert Cecil concerning the state of that Province, he reported (including doubtless the last mentioned sufferings recalled by Moryson above):

About the 5th Oct., some 3,000 rebels came into the county of Limerick, sent from the archtraitor Tyrone, under the leading of John FitzThomas...elder brother to the last attainted Earl of Desmond...and burnt and spoiled most of the towns and villages there...These combinations and revolts have effected many execrable murders and cruelties upon the English, as well in the county of Limerick, as in the counties of Cork and Kerry, and elsewhere; infants taken from their nurses' breasts, and the brains dashed against the walls; the heart plucked out of the body of the husband in the view of the wife, who was forced to yield the use of her apron to wipe off the blood from the murderer's fingers, [an] English gentleman at midday in a town cruelly murdered, and his head cleft in divers pieces; divers sent into Youghal amongst the English, some with their throats cut, but not killed, some with their tongues cut out of their heads, others with their noses cut off; by view whereof the English might the more bitterly lament the misery of their countrymen, and fear the like to befall to themselves.

In 1599 the Queen sent over another of her favourites, the Earl of Essex, with a large army of 20,000 men, to quell the rebellion and stop the Spanish landings. But he abysmally and totally mismanaged the affair, and after dissipating his fine army he left the country in a worse state than he found it. He was to be replaced by Lord Mountjoy, who was to reduce the Irish chiefs to submission, and route a force of 4,000 Spanish infantry in 1601.

The widespread destruction was not all one-sided. The government troops also indulged in wholesale and systematic destruction of crops and food in order to exterminate the peasantry by famine.

During 1599 there are several mentions of Sir Arthur Champernowne in *CSPI*, in relation to the army at Leinster, *viz.* 21 August, 16 October, 29 October, and 10 November. In August he was on the Council of the Army as a colonel (*CSPI*, page 127). He had been knighted on 12 July 1598 by the Earl of Essex in Ireland during the Revolt, but was said to have died there in November 1599, probably of the widespread sickness amongst the forces there. These details however cannot at present be reconciled with the Champernowne Pedigree.

POST-1598 MUNSTER REBELLION

There was little change in Munster for 18 months after the 1598 rising. But with the arrival in January 1600 of William, Lord Mountjoy as Lord Deputy of Ireland, and Sir George Carew as Lord President of Munster with Crown forces, the Irish rebels, under O'Neill, Earl of Tyrone, began to lose ground, including county Kerry. Also in 1600 Boyle left London to return to Ireland to serve under Carew, who appointed him clerk of the Munster council, a post previously held by the late Edmund Spenser. John Champernowne of Modbury was to marry Catherine, daughter of Lord Mountjoy.

Many seignories were sold to other undertakers. Boyle was now clerk of the Munster council, appointed by Sir George Carew in 1600. Several army men were lessees of lands who had to be bought out by Boyle in these and other seignories.

In 1600 woods covered one eighth of the country, though because of gradual clearance there was beginning to be a lack of mature timber. These woods were used by rebels as hiding places for themselves and their cattle. This denuding was to lead to decline and eventually loss of some indigenous fauna, such as wolves. Dingle was now a beautiful but remote Kerry fishing-village, though of primary importance with a merchant population and a municipal organisation. It sustained important commercial links with Bristol and Bordeaux. Visitors noted the massively built houses and the splendid main street, with gates at each end to be opened and closed in time of war.

<u>26 October 1600</u> At Dublin:

A Breviate of grants passed by Her Majesty's warrant to servitors in Ireland, since the 20th year of Her Majesty's reign [including] John Champen,

<u>6 June 1601.</u> Dublin. The Council of Ireland wrote to Sir George Carew that Thomas Smyth, commissary of the victuals for Connaught had complained

that having sent one Captain Francis Gode to Bordeaux to bring from thence to Galway...a barque loaden with Bordeaux wines, and the same being accordingly provided, the said Gode...contrary to the charter partly discharged the said wines at Dinglecushe, and having received 92*l* [£92] sterling in money for part of the same, one Champion, supposed Vice-Admiral of those parts, with force,..with others, took away the said money from him together with £20, 10s, 0d from one John Butler a merchant of Galway alleging the same to be forfeited as money bound for foreign countries...we pray you see that Campion and the rest be compelled to restore the money to Smyth and Butler. (*Cal. Carew Mss IV, 1601-1603*, page 81.)

28 June 1602. Sir George Carew was in turn to write to Secretary Sir Robert Cecil:

I wish that Ireland were a fish pool, for this age shall never see it settled in peace...God once deliver me from this hydra's task, where toil and mischiefs are endless. (*Cal. Carew Mss IV* page 258)

By November 1602 there were only a few areas of resistance - with very small rebel bands in Kerry. But not before English settlers had been murdered, or mostly driven off leaving everything they owned behind, and the Plantation had therefore been comprehensively destroyed and re-occupied by the previous Irish tenants, etc.

Again there was to be wholesale and systematic countrywide destruction of crops and food by English forces in order to exterminate the peasantry by famine. Sir George Carew followed this practice from the beginning, and again Munster was to be brought to a state as dreadful as after the previous Desmond Rebellion twenty years earlier.

After the Rebellion had been quashed undertakers were urged to go back onto their lands, but many of them and their settlers had gone back to England, or were now too poor. Some did return, but to damaged or destroyed accommodation.

1602/1604 Boyle obtained a patent grant from King James for the purchase of Ralegh's 3½ seignories in co. Cork and co. Waterford, apparently for the knock-down price of £1,000. Sir George Carew acted as intermediary. Boyle was able to obtain further patent grants in turn for other lands. Much of Munster woodland had been felled by Boyle for fuelling his Irish ironworks, the export of planks and pipe-staves to France, and ship-building in England. By 1608 the best timber had gone to France; and by the late 1620s other enterprises had to end because of a fuel shortage due to Boyle's short-sighted failure to renew felled timber by coppicing.

25 July 1603 Sir George Carew had been able to negotiate the second marriage for the now widowed Boyle, to the daughter of Sir Geoffrey Fenton, the Plantation surveyor, and also procured a knighthood bestowed the same day.

1606 John Champion sold whole of his seignory of Ballymacdonnell to Sir Richard Boyle. (*Lismore 2,1*, pages 97, 182-189.) *Burke's*, etc. say this sale was in 1603, and that the sale price was £26,400 which was large for those days - especially as compared with what was paid for the much larger Ralegh seignory. Champion/Chapman supposedly lived for eight years after this transaction. See 10 August 1611 below.

July 1606/1607 Amongst the Crown lands and Tithes in Ireland now in lease from King James I were:

co. Gallway - John Champen, the chapel of Killmurry.
co. Kerry - Assigns of Jo. Champen, lands of the abbey of Ratowth alias Arragacensis, of the order of St Augustin, and of the late abbey of Oderny, alias Ladies Abbey, of Keriolezen [*Kyrie Eleison*].
co. Cork - Jo. Champen, the rectory of Ballinter and Esibacke.
co. Roscommon - Jo. Champen, land near the town of Higgins called Monasterevan alias Kennett late possession of the monastery of Nenaghe [which latter is in co. Tipperary, 19 miles N.E. of Limerick].

This tallies with the previous allocation of lands and properties enumerated in Chapter 4.

1607 A Thomas Champion was High Sheriff of co. Kerry.
1610 A Richard Chapman was bound in recognizance for Richard Reynard, yeoman of Mozeely. (*BM 697 f74v*)

Hickson in her *Old Kerry Records, 2nd Series*, said regarding the Patent of 1588/1589 to John Champion and George Stone:

By a Chancery Inquisition taken at the "Island of Kyery" (i.e. Castleisland) the 10th of August, 1611, it would appear that Stone conveyed his interest to Champion, who in turn conveyed to Sir Richard Boyle, his heirs and assigns for ever, to his and their uses.

And then in MacCarthy-Morrogh's thesis, dealing with the same Inquisition, it was initially thought that pay dirt had really been struck:

10 August 1611 'By a Chancery Inquisition taken in Kerry on this day, and preserved in the National Archives of Ireland, it appears that John Champion, or Champernowne, and George Stone had a grant from Queen Elizabeth of the whole barony of Corcaguiny, the western portion of the rebel Earl of Desmond's forfeited palatinate of Kerry; that this barony was divided into two districts, Corcaguiny proper and Litteragh; that Stone conveyed his interest therein to Champion, who in turn conveyed the whole barony to Sir Richard Boyle, his heirs and assigns for ever.'

But when a copy hand-written transcription of this Inquisition was examined at the National Archives of Ireland (Ref. *RC 4/7*), the following was found:

Inquisition at the Island of Kyery aka Mountegle in the Countie of Kerry on 10 August 1611 and in Nynth year of James...The said Jurors Doe fynde and present that John Champion and Geordge Stonne were joint pattentees of the part or porcion of a Signiory called Balli mcDonnell in the Countie of Kyery who being jointly seized thereof the said Geordge Stone did convey his Moytie and whole interest [two spaces] lands contained in their joint Pattent to John Champion and his heires for ever who entered and being soly seised in his demeasne as of fee of the said Ballym'Donnell and the rest of the lands and tennements in the same trẽs pattents contained conveyed the same to Sir Richard Boyle Knight his heires and assignes for ever to his and their sole and proper use, And the said Sir Richard Boyle hath estated the underwritten persons as freeholders [farmers] and tennentes in the severall landes ensuing and for the severall estates underwritten, vizt-

Lease of Ballinecourtie, Manegarand, Comeduff, Killgane, Bynnarter & Ballentermon contg CCL acres of land, - stone house newly built.
Latimore & Ballihoa contg CCL acres of land,
Town & lands of Balligahill & Letrynne being of the Mc Edmondes land contg CCCC acres of land, with dwelling house erected upon Balligahill,
Town & lands of Ballinesitor & Churchtowne contg C acres of land and a good house built thereupon,
Part Land of Ballin McDonnell contg C acres, with house built,
Lands of Killalownes part of BallinMcDonnell contg C acres of land & a smaller tenement built thereupon,
Town & lands of Downkyne contg C acres & a small tenement built thereupon,
Town & lands of Ballineigh contg C acres on which a house built,

but no freeholders or tenants were listed.

Thus contrary to what McCarthy-Morrogh stated there is no mention of Champernowne - not in this copy transcript at any rate. But at least here is the official record of the sale to the Earl of Cork of those same lands and properties earlier granted to John Champen/Champion/etc., to substantiate the proposition that these were really one and the same person.

The reason for the sale is not given, or guessed at, but judging by Herbert's comment of 13 September 1589 regarding Stone's and Champen's "insufficient means", the litigation by Herbert, plus the 1598 Revolution, it is no wonder that Chapman wanted to get shot of his lands. Ranger has said that although it was possible to buy land more advantageously in Ireland than in England, Boyle was prepared to pay at high rates for land he particularly wanted. Thus the alleged (and unverified) generous price of £26,400 paid to John Chapman (equivalent to around £3,000,000 at present values), would have been an offer he could not refuse. The fate of Ralegh thus seems not to have had any bearing on the matter as stated in *Burke* and *Debrett*. Chapman did seemingly however retain certain non-landed leases.

30 August 1611:

The Names of English Tenants and the Inhabitants of Sir Richard Boyles Plantation which were viewed and mustered at Tullow, the 30th of August 1611 before Sir Richard Moryson, Knt, Vice-President...Pikemen, armed:-...John Champion... (*Cal. Carew Mss, Vol. 6, 1603-1624*)

Would this be a son of either the original John or William Chapman?

In *Grosart I, Vol. 1*, page 233, is the following entry of Richard Boyle, dated around this period:

I gaue M^r doughty of Bristoll order by my letters to pay Mr John phillips and Marie his wyffe, widdoe, and Adminstrtrix to hercules Strowbridge of Bristoll, merchant, 20^li ster:, out of the moneys M^r doughty had of myne in his hands for Sow Iron, in regard that M^r phillips delivered me certen deeds of the Lands M^r peepes is my tenant vnto in Kerry; which Mr John Champon had passed to the said Hercules Strowbridge and one Mr Roe of London, draper, and this 20^li I paid him at thinstance of my lo : president, Sir Edw Harrys, Mr John Whitson of Bristoll, & Cap^n Robert Tynt.

This was an example of the roundabout way Boyle raised cash to acquire lands.

1611 An 'Abstract of Inquisitions' to be found in the *CSPI* concerning the then present state of lands undertaken in Munster, reads:

A part of a seignory called Bally M'Donnell granted to John Champion and George Stone; the King's now tenant Sir Richard Boyle, whereof-
Demesnes - 250 acres
Fee farms - 250 acres

Leases, 6 - 900 acres
Small tenures, 14
Rent reserved £36.0s.6½d
Rent payable £36.0s.6½d
Breaches of the Articles of Plantation found by Inquisition-
Some Irish undertenants are dwelling in this seignory.
Mustered for this seignory - Horse 6, Foot 13.

4 October 1611 In an

'Abstract of the Undertakers of Mounster [*sic*], their horse and foot, mustered and presented before me Sir Richard Moryson, Knight, Vice-President,...For the seignory of Stone and Champion in the possession, of Sir Richard Boyle, 6 Horse and 13 foot. (*Cal. Carew Mss, Vol. 6, 1603-1624*)

January 1613 King James I confirmed to Sir Richard Boyle his rights to Munster lands, including:

...ffrom John Champon, deceased, the Mannor our Signory of Bally m[c] Daniell and other Landes and tenements in our countie of Kerrie, whereof the said Sir Richard and his Tennants are now quietly possessed. (*Grosart II, Vol. 1*, page 184)

1616 In the Ballymacdonell seignory there was a recorded total of 15-21 English tenants and undertenants. (Inquisitions *PROI 1A/48/59, 64, 66, 69.*) Whether these figures were the number of families is not clear. An accepted average is of 5 persons per family/household. It was still underpopulated, as were other seignories.

July 1617 A Charles Champernowne surrendered his old lease of the Charoon(?), and took on a new one off Richard Boyle, reserving woods to Boyle. He appears to pay £5 per annum. (*Grosart 1.1.159 & 212*)

1619 *Lismore Volume I*, page xxv - Letter to the Earl of Cork (late Sir Richard Boyle):

John Chapman's Relation of Proceedings in Star-Chamber against Earl of Suffolk & Sir John Binglye [in London, December 1619. Account ends],..your Lordship the offices of an humbled frend as I am, in shorte your lordships servant

CHAPMAN.

1620 *Lismore Volume II*, pages 168-180. Another letter to Earl of Cork, from London:

29 Junij 1620 ffrom Mr. John Chapman.
This paper will bear comparison with others used by historians. It tempts keenly to discussion of men and opinions.

This Chapman, whoever he might have been, considered he and Cork to be on good loving terms.

1621 A John Chapman had gone to Turkey. (*Grosart 1.2.21*) Trade with Turkey had been steadily pressed forward under Elizabeth, as it had been under Henry VIII. In June 1580, The Charter of Liberties to English merchants in Turkey had been formally issued. A year later certain disorders committed by English freebooters in the Levant were redressed. In 1586 five London ships from Turkey had to fight their way through the Straits of Gibraltar against some Spanish vessels.

1622 A John Chapman was a leaseholder on a Norris seignory, of 30 acres. (Thomas Norris had been an undertaker at Mallow, Munster, in 1589)

End of 1625: In the *CSPI*, amongst the List of Officers that came out of Ireland may be found

"Ensign Champernoone."

THE CHAPMAN GRANT IN COUNTY WESTMEATH UNDER THE ACTS OF SETTLEMENT

JOHN CHAMPERNPOWNE/CHAMPION/CHAMPEN/CHAPMAN c.1560-c.1613. It has been seen that he was granted lands in Kerry 1586, which were subsequently sold to Earl of Cork in 1606. "He lived eight years after this transaction, leaving at his decease, his brother William Chapman." There is no knowledge of John having been married, though one or two members of the present extended Chapman family in the USA and West Indies thought at one time this might have been possible. This lack of subsequent direct descendant family is somewhat confirmed by subsequent comment from these same members. But as was noted earlier, Charles Smith ambiguously quoted in his book regarding John Chapman and his partner John Stone 'neither of whose posterity in the male line remain in this county [Kerry]'. Did this mean that there may have been at least marriages, with perhaps daughters? Though it has been noted that Hickson had said (without substantiation) there was some continuity of genealogy between the two generations of John and Benjamin Chapman.

WILLIAM CHAPMAN c.1560-c.1620. Nothing is really known about him, and certainly no knowledge of any family. Others had assumed he had a son, though seemingly incorrectly stated (see below) to have been the Captain Benjamin Chapman below. Was he the William Chapman stated earlier to have been a vice-constable of Dungarvan Castle in April 1589?

<u>1649</u> In O'Hart's *Irish and Anglo-Irish Landed Gentry* when Cromwell came to Ireland, there are two mentions of Chapmans. Firstly, on page 266 there is a THOMAS CHAPMAN listed as one of 35 forfeiting papist proprietors whose lands were confiscated in the Barony of Shelburne (or Shelbourne), in the south-west of co. Wexford. Then on page 455 there is a BENJAMIN CHAPMAN mentioned in the grants made under the Acts of Settlement and Explanation.

Although these two items are at first glance disconnected, the second is an example of a consequence of the first action; or putting it another way, for the second to occur the first had to take place. It is thus appropriate to follow in some detail the events and circumstances under which Benjamin Chapman might have obtained his supposed Westmeath estate. This Benjamin (c.1620-1680), if related, was possibly a son, but more probably likely to have been grandson of either the original John or William Chapman.

Benjamin had entered as a cornet into a cavalry regiment raised by the Earl of Inchiquin (Murrough O'Brien 1614-1674) for Parliament. He would not then have been the 'Ensign Champernowne' of 1625 above, since the cavalry equivalent to the infantry 'ensign' would be 'cornet'.

Inchiquin's father (a Gaelic Protestant royalist) had died while he was still a minor, and custody of his property was under Sir William St.Leger, lord president of Munster, whose daughter Inchiquin was to marry. He was to return in 1639 from Spanish service in Italy. Appointed Vice-President of Munster 1640, and an M.P. With the outbreak of the 1641 rebellion in Ulster he was part of St.Leger's expedition against the rebels.

With St.Leger's death in July 1642 Inchiquin became governor of Munster. Although he co-operated with Richard Boyle and his sons in their actions against the rebels, it was not done cordially. In 1643 much of his force was ordered to England to serve the king, and being scattered under various leaders. In a fashion he defected in 1644 to the Parliamentarians, who made him President of Munster, where he continued to aggressively (even harshly) fight against the Irish. But in early 1648 the 'disreputable' Inchiquin rejoined the Royalists, and captured Drogheda for the Royalists until it was finally recaptured by Cromwell in the September. Meanwhile, some of his officers had deserted to Parliament, and he began to lose his powerful influence, though still able to recruit forces against the Parliamentarians. In 1650 he went to France, being appointed to the exiled Charles II's royal council. He was reported by the parliamentarians as trying to raise a revolt in Munster. In the Cromwellian Act of Settlement, 12 August 1652, Inchiquin was excepted by name from pardon for life or estate. After the Restoration a private Act was passed in September 1660 which restored him all his honours and lands in Ireland, and this was confirmed by the Act of Settlement of 1662. He was created Earl of Inchiquin in 1654. He converted to Catholicism in 1656, though his wife remained Protestant.

In 1667, as Captain Chapman, Benjamin is said (in *Grand Juries of Westmeath from 1727*) to have obtained from Oliver Cromwell the grant by certificate of a large estate of St. Lucy's, co. Westmeath, and resided there the rest of his life. St. Lucy's had formerly been a Preceptory or cell of the medieval religious order of the Knights Hospitallers of St. John of Jerusalem. This grant was presumably for services rendered during Commander-in-Chief Cromwell's suppression of the Irish Rebellion in 1649-1650 - but Cromwell had died in 1658, aged 59.

Returning to the purely historical aspect, Patents for a Plantation in county Westmeath and elsewhere had been granted as far back as 1621.

In October 1641 a rebellion of the Irish flared in Ulster, soon to be joined by Old English; and rebels quickly controlled the whole of Ireland, except for some heavily defended towns, or some gentry in their castles.

Then in 1642 had been passed the Adventurer's Act and other subsequent Acts of Subscription which allowed sufficiently affluent Englishmen to contribute towards the cost of conquering Ireland. These costs included the pay of the contracted 10,000 soldiers recruited to quell this latest Irish rebellion. The English Parliament approved the raising of £1 million on the security of 2½ million acres of Irish land, to be forfeited after the rebellion. These investing adventurers were guaranteed Irish estates and manors at the end of the war. These would be of 1,000 acres for £200 in Ulster (at the yearly Rent of £4 4s. 4d or about 1d per acre), £450 in Munster (yearly Rent £9 1s. 6d or about 2d per acre), and £600 in Leinster; with lands proportionately for lesser sums. Cromwell was one such adventurer, and was eventually granted land. As Lord

Protector, from 1653 he was to supervise the implementation of these and subsequent Acts, for what was to become known as the Cromwellian plantation. An Ordinance of 1643 also allowed officers of the army to become adventurers to the extent of their pay, i.e. land in lieu of pay.

Later in 1642 was 'An Act for determining the accompts of such officers and soldiers as are or have been employed in the service of the Commonwealth in Ireland'. The was to describe a means for officers and soldiers, who were owed back pay, to receive debentures for grants "out of rebel lands, houses, tenements and hereditaments in Ireland or other lands, houses, tenements and hereditaments there in dispose of the Commonwealth of England."

The Adventurer's Act had been passed to stop the King having his own army to send to Ireland to quell the rebellion, which when done could then be returned to go against Parliament. Thus the offer of 2,500,000 acres of forfeited Irish land was security for the raising and paying of a private army over which the King had no control - except to sign the officers' commissions. But Parliament was just as bad, and used the army thus raised to fight in England against the King, and it was not until 1649 that it eventually went to Ireland under Cromwell, who was there from August 1649 to May 1650 as civil and military Governor of Ireland. When he left Henry Ireton took over, and carried out the Cromwellian settlement with some vigour for the next year or so. It was not until September 1653 that the Irish rebellion was declared by Parliament as having been subdued.

In 1647, Lord Inchiquin, Vice-President of Munster, had been in trouble for filling deserted houses and farms in Munster with his own servants, and staff. His reply being that he did that to preserve the properties which might otherwise become derelict.

With the execution of Charles I in January 1649 there were many reasons for taking the offensive in suppressing Ireland, e.g. a large Commonwealth army was in existence with many of its soldiers still owed money for services rendered, and the Adventurer's Act had to be honoured.

There were the Inrolments of the Adjudicators in favour of the 1649 Officers (many of Irish origin), formerly denominated "The '49 Lots". These refer to the arrears of the Commissioned Officers who served Charles I or Charles II, in the Wars of Ireland, before 5 June 1649. O'Hart has listed these, and amongst those named were 'John Champeon, William Champeon, John Champion, William Champion, Thomas Chapman'. John and William are more than likely to be duplicated names. Can all three be considered the missing links between the original John and William and the later Benjamin?

The Battle of Worcester in September 1651 saw the defeat of the Prince of Wales, the future Charles II, and thus ended the English Civil War.

Royalist landowners, under the 1652 'Act for the Settling of Ireland' both Protestant and Catholic throughout Ireland were now to be relieved of their lands, which passed to English Adventurers as a reward for their earlier speculation, and also to Parliamentary soldiers (particularly officers) whose pay was in arrears. In September 1653, by which time the land was deemed sufficiently depopulated to allow the English to occupy it, under the 'Act for the speedy and effectual Satisfaction of the Adventurers for Lands in Ireland, and of the Arrears due to the Soldiery there and of other public debts and for the Encouragement of Protestants to Plant and inhabit Ireland', which determined how much officers and soldiers were owed in back pay.

There was a survey and allocation of forfeited Irish lands, followed by arrangements for transplanting and transportation of the displaced landowners. This was firstly 'beyond the Shannon' to the Province of Connaught and co. Clare in N.W. Ireland, of nobility and gentry, i.e. those with substantial landed property, with the labouring classes generally excluded. Connaught was then the most wasted Province in Ireland, and almost surrounded by the sea and River Shannon. But a narrow strip along the seaboard was allocated to adventurers, etc., further hemming in the Irish transplanted. Thus this form of internment (similar to an American Indian Reservation, or 'ethnic cleansing' in modern parlance) could be easily managed. Escape from which brought a liability to trial by military court and sentence of death. Many of these transplanted went to the West Indies, where it was possible there were 12,000 Irish by the late 1660s.

By the end of August 1653 some 10,000 disbanded soldiers were drifting round Ireland, waiting for a land grant in lieu of back pay. Then by September 1654 there were a further 5,000.

Allocation of land to adventurers and soldiers was by lottery. Firstly, to decide in which Province, then again in which county. It was thus seemingly pure chance that Benjamin's regiment drew the Province of Leinster (in which is co. Westmeath) rather than those of Munster or Ulster in the lottery. Lots in county Westmeath were not to exceed £70,000 in value. A 1650s £1 would be somewhat equivalent to £100 in 2000. In Leinster soldiers were to have 1,600 English acres (1,000 Irish acres) for every £600 of arrears, i.e. 12 shillings per acre. But this blanket valuation was considered by the soldiery to be anomalous regarding the comparative values of land in the several counties. Some were more fertile than others, or some much less so. Equalising valuation adjustments were accordingly made, and in county Westmeath the valuation rose from £600 to £900 per 1,600 English acres - presumably because of its higher fertility and/or potential. Benjamin Chapman would thus have received less land than he might have at first anticipated. Westmeath was also one of the counties where grants were to be divided such that adventurers and soldiers were to be inter-mixed for safety purposes.

But there were to be further likewise equalising revaluations of the baronies. Delvin barony, in which is St. Lucy's/Killua, was set out to "Colnell Ingoldsby's Regiment - His own Troope" at £800 per 1,600 English acres. Yet even then there was to be still further equalisation between the individual plots.

Was Captain Benjamin Chapman one of the officers who left the service of Inchiquin, and did he enter into Ingoldby's regiment, and thus take pot luck in the lotting; or was his property such that it was granted separately?

Neither Inchiquin, Chapman nor Ingoldsby are mentioned in Peacock's *The Army Lists of the Roundheads and Cavaliers of 1642* - either in mainland Britain or for the 'Irish Expedition under command of Philip, Lord Wharton'. Therefore it may be assumed that they were all in Ireland by that date, or not yet commissioned. Colonel Henry Ingoldsby (1622-1701), the younger brother of Colonel Richard Ingoldsby, commanded a regiment in Ireland under Cromwell and Henry Ireton. In September 1654 'the remainder of his regiment of dragoons were disbanded', but early in 1656 he was still on active service in Ireland against the Quakers. He represented the counties of Kerry, Limerick, and Clare in Cromwell's parliaments of 1654, 1656 and 1659. In the latter county he was to be personally granted land. In 1659 he was Governor of Limerick, and a supporter of Richard Cromwell as Lord Protector; but that same year he fled to France. He was created a baronet by both Lord Protector Cromwell in 1658, and Charles II in 1660.

The young Dr. (later Sir) William Petty (1623-1687), Physician-General to the Army, came to Ireland in 1652 and was responsible for the survey. It became known as the 'Down Survey' because of Petty's continued reference to it as "by survey laid down", or "laid down by admeasurement". He became as a consequence very rich, having bought up many land debentures from soldiers, and in suspect deals - becoming in the process a second Sir Richard Boyle of fifty years previously.

At lotting the soldiers' debentures (in which were declared the amount of arrears of pay due) were exchanged for certificates declaring the amount of the debenture and the number of acres in the barony to satisfy it. Upon getting possession the half pay of officers and soldiers ceased. Those with only small allotments (both ordinary soldiers and officers) often sold out to those with larger. Many being unable to subsist on their pay, and being distressed, were often forced to sell their debentures, perhaps at a considerable discount. Then officers might cheat or exploit further their soldiers (or each other) when planting by showing them a bog or grossly inferior land, which they then exchanged for a pittance.

But once on their lands these soldiers had no ploughs or horses, nor money to buy them; and any potential Irish workforce had either been transplanted or were in hiding. Amongst the latter were the discontented or outlawed Irish who were to harass and murder English settlers.

Amongst the transplanted nobility and gentry Irish were also the doctors, merchants, tradesmen and artisans that the English adventurers could not afford to lose, as there was not much in the way of comparable English replacement to start with.

But perhaps more serious was a shortage of women, for there were dire penalties for what was considered high treason for anyone to take an Irish girl for a wife unless she had first genuinely professed Protestantism. Well into the 18th century a Protestant who married a Catholic, and she did not conform to the English religion within a year, he became 'a constructive Papist', and could be treated worse that an actual Papist, including being deprived of all rights. This may partly account for T. E. Lawrence's comment that the Chapman's only married their own kind. But with a continued lack of English women it was inevitable that the majority of soldiers and officers would marry Irish women, in spite of all restrictions and harsh penalties - which the authorities were generally unable to enforce.

The lists of these individual sub-divisions were sent at the Restoration (1660) to the Commissioners for executing the Act of Settlement, but these were unfortunately amongst the historical documents destroyed in the great fire of 1711 at the Council Office in Dublin. Then in the Four Courts there was a manuscript volume:*Accounts of Soldiers stated singly*. O'Hart only quoted one such account, which gave men's rank, company, regiment, dates of period of service, and amount of arrears; with in the case of a dead soldier the name of his wife.

As the land was not yet quite subdued it was arranged that civilian and soldier adventurers be intermixed in their respective baronies. Amongst the Cromwellian and Restoration lands confiscated between 1653-1565, some 75%

of Westmeath was confiscated and assigned to adventurers and soldiers.

Between 1651 and 1654, as well as the transplanting of landed nobility and gentry to Connaught, some 40,000 Irish soldiers who did not wish to be transplanted in Ireland went to Spain and other European states. Whilst thousands of widows, plus deserted wives of departed soldiers, young girls and boys, orphans and destitutes were rounded up, or seized from their homes, and transported to sugar plantations in the West Indies (particularly Barbados), and to English Plantations in America as a form of slave trade.

Colonel Richard Lawrence, the governor of Waterford, was to recall:

> About the year 1652 and 1653 the plague and famine had so swept away whole counties that a man might travel twenty or thirty miles and not see a living creature, either man, beast or bird, they being either all dead or had quit those desolate places; or soldiers would tell stories of the place where they saw a smoke; it was so rare to see either smoke by day or fire or candle by night. And when we did meet with two or three poor cabins, none but very aged men and women and children, and those, like the prophet, might have complained; We are become as a bottle in the smoke; our skin is black like an oven, because of the terrible famine. I have seen those miserable creatures plucking stinking, rotten carrion out of a ditch, black and rotten, and been credibly informed that they dug corpses out of the grave to eat.

Cities and towns were desolate of inhabitants, but with traitors' and rebels' heads on spikes no uncommon sight. Plague, famine, emigration and transplantation was to be responsible for $^5/_6$ of the Irish population. Wolves were as a consequence to multiply, and become more of a problem. To encourage the hunting of them, rewards were given of £6 for the head of a bitch wolf, £5 of a dog wolf, and for that of a cub from ten shilling to £2.

Ireland was now divided into three: 1. Connaught for transplanted Irish only. 2. East side of Ireland for pure English (and Protestant foreignors) only, without a single Irish servant or tenant. This area stretched from Drogheda in the north, and bounded by the sea and the Rivers Boyne and Barrow down to Waterford in the south. 3. The area in between, which included Westmeath, was to be a mixed plantation, where any authorised Irish were to be turned into genuine Protestant English in all senses of the word. Some original Irish landowners became tenants of Adventurers on what had previously been their own land. But with these tenancies,plus inevitable inter-marriage, etc. the 'English only' and 'mixed' areas again became increasing Irish.

As Prendergast wrote, regarding 1654:

Such was the national hatred of the Royalists of England to the Irish (who fought, and lost country and everything for the King), that even in their common exile abroad they rejoiced at Cromwell's proceedings in stripping the Irish of their lands."

In June 1657 came the Settlement Act 'for the Assuming, Confirming and Settling of Lands and Estates in Ireland', and Act for Convicting, Discovering and Repressing of Popish Recusants. This was followed in 1662 by the 'Act of Settlement', which gave the Crown the right to reorganise the disposition of all confiscated lands, except those held by the Church or Trinity College, confirming some adventurers' landowning rights, but also allowing claims from 'innocents' and royalist supporters. 'Innocents', whoever they were, could repossess without arranging compensation for those who had dispossessed them, but the Act was not to be implemented to any substantial degree. Then there was the Act of Explanation in 1665.

Sir William Petty had estimated at the time that the population of Ireland in 1641 was 1,448,000 - of which 504,000 were native Irish had perished by 1652. Within a few years another 40,000 young Irish men had gone abroad for service in European countries, and that another 100,000 of men, women and children were transported to the colonies and Americas. Petty's census of 1659 calculated the total population of all Ireland as 500,091. In spite of all the transportation, transplanting, etc., the ratio of English to Irish and others was still only 1:7.

Cromwell, the Lord Protector, was to die on 3 September 1658, to be followed briefly by his eldest son, Richard. Under the Act for the Settlement of Ireland, passed after King Charles II's Restoration in May 1660, innocent Papists were to be restored, and dispossessed soldiers to be reprised. Some old English gentry who had lost their estates were able to retrieve them.

If 1667 was the correct date of captain Benjamin Chapman's grant, and not a misprint for 1657, Charles II was legally bound to honour any adventurer's or soldier's certificate issued under the authority of someone who had signed Charles I's death warrant, or had fought on that person's side? According to Tom Reilly in a letter to the author:

"...the plantation policy of the Commonwealth government was eagerly adopted by Charles II, The main reason for this was because unlike other earlier attempts at colonisation of the entire island of Ireland this one actually worked,"

The Acts of Settlement 14 & 15 of Charles II in 1662, confirmed some adventurers' landowning rights but also allowing claims from 'innocents' and royalist supporters. ll lands in the possession of Cromwellian financiers (adventurers) before May 1659 were secure in them; as were some other claimants who were satisfied or compensated. Therefore native Irish were generally greatly upset at the general confirmation of the Cromwellian confiscatiobs. But many colonists were gradually being absorbed and becoming Irish, thus helping to preserve the Irish culture - that is until the coming of William of Orange, when it would all start again.

The transportation scheme had not really been a success, for after the Restoration those banished to Connaught and co. Clare started to return to claim their estates and lands. Presumably Benjamin Chapman was secure in his property, being what it had been originally. Still to be ascertained, however, was any definite date and method by which he acquired the estate.

CHAPMAN LATER FORTUNES IN IRELAND

Captain **BENJAMIN CHAPMAN** (not known when born, but considered by the author to be c.1610) is said to have married (c.1650) Anne, daughter of Robert Parkinson of Ardee, co. Louth by whom he had it is believed three sons, and possibly a daughter.

WILLIAM: c.1650-1734 (see below);

Thomas: c.1653 - . Went "to America", i.e. Barbados, West Indies, where he settled (according to members of the Chapman family. There was already a land-owning Thomas Chapman there in 1638. Matthew, Richard, and John, grandsons of Benjamin, who were land and slave owners in Barbados around 1650s or 1660s, all indicated in their will that they were "of Ireland". Another family belief is that "there were three Chapman brothers" and that their "kin" was Captain Benjamin Chapman. (After Cromwell's final capture of Drogheda in 1649, some prisoners were shipped off to "the Barbadoes".)

Samuel: c.1655 - . He was taught by a Mr Neal (possibly a private tutor). On 28 April 1673, when aged 17, Samuel entered Trinity College, Dublin, as a Pensioner - as "son of Benjamin Chapman, Gentleman". (A pensioner was someone who paid a fixed sum annually: therefore of parents of moderate income.)

Catherine: c.1671-1728. Married 28 January 1695 to William Copeland of Kilrush, said to have been a priest hunter during the age of the Penal Laws (1691-1778), for which the Chapmans have also been accused of doing. She died 14 February 1728, aged 56 years, and was buried in Killua cemetery, where there is a memorial slab.

In the *Census of Ireland c.1659* there is shown a Benjamin Chapman, gent, (who would have qualified to be so-called as an ex-officer, and presumed heir to the fortune made by the earlier sale of the Munster properties), at Killuah, where there was in total 2 English and 59 Irish people. According to *The Book of Surveys and Distribution of the Estates of the County of Westmeath Forfeited in the Year*

1641, the proprietor shown by the 1640 Civil Survey was Richard Nugent, 1st Earl of Westmeath (c.1585-1641). Land profitable being 723 acres 2 rods 4 perches. These acres were disposed on the Acts by the Down Survey:

718 acres 2 rods 0 perches to Benjamin Chapman by Certificate dated 16 September 1667.

005 acres 0 rods 2 perches to William Deacon by Certificate dated 26 December 1667.

BENJAMIN, was later said to be admitted to Grays Inn, London.
It is not known when he died, but he was to be succeeded by his son WILLIAM (c.1650-1734).

Nothing apparently is known about the original St. Lucy property at Clonmellon at that time, and probably never will be. The first purpose built house would not be until the 18th century.

A successor Nugent (Catholics) could be said as being responsible for Colonel Ingoldsby's Regiment being allowed settlement in Delvin barony. The Regiment was camped in front of Nugent's castle there. Cromwell said he was intending to stay at the castle, but Nugent said he would rather burn the castle down, which he proceeded to do. This had been the second castle on the site, the ruins of which are now on Delvin golf-course. The third, Clonyn Castle, is now a private residence.

WILLIAM CHAPMAN: c.1650-1734

Elder son of Captain BENJAMIN CHAPMAN above.
1697 and 1698. As "William Chapman, Gentleman" was a Commissioner for raising a supply in the county of Westmeath.
1703. In the *magna panella* as "Willus Chapman de Killua, Gen." (*Grand Juries of Westmeath*)
1727. On the Grand Jury of Westmeath.
Married Ismay, daughter of Thomas Nugent of Clonlost, probably related to the Earls of Westmeath. They had sons:

- **BENJAMIN**: c.1700-1779 (see below).
- William: Born c.1711 at Killua. Educated by a Mr Johnston of Dublin. 10 July 1727 entered Trinity College, Dublin, as a Pensioner, aged 16. B.A. in Spring 1732. Called to the Irish Bar 1740. 1772-1781 possibly on the Grand Jury of Westmeath.

Died 1734, 'of Killua', being succeeded by his son BENJAMIN.

In *Eton College Lists 1678-1790* (which very rarely shows initials or first names) there appears an unidentifiable Chapman in 1706 (as a Colleger), and in 1707. These dates do not appear to tally with the family members mentioned here, and thus may be of another branch.

Trinity College, Dublin, had been founded by Queen Elizabeth in 1591; and from about 1650 until 1793 admission was to be confined to Protestants. Between 1600-1700 Trinity College was granted confiscated lands in Kerry. Thus it for quite some time received rents from Catholics to solely educate Protestants.

BENJAMIN CHAPMAN: c.1700-1779

Eldest son of WILLIAM CHAPMAN (c.1650-1734) above.
1718. In the *Eton College Lists* there is an unidentifiable Chapman shown as a Colleger in the Fourth Form, who could well be this family member.
1729. On Grand Jury of Westmeath.
1733. High Sheriff of co. Meath.
1734. Succeeded his father William.
1751. High Sheriff of Westmeath.
c.1740 married Anne, daughter of Robert Tighe (1682-1766) & Anne (née Clements) of Mitchelstown, near Delvin, co. Westmeath. They had three sons and two daughters, including:

BENJAMIN: c.1745-1810 (see below).
THOMAS: 1756-1837 (see below).

1733 served as High Sheriff of co. Meath.
1734 succeeded his father at Killua.
1751 served as High Sheriff of co. Westmeath.
1763 on Grand Jury of Westmeath.
31 October 1768 date of will (proved in Ireland 9 August 1779).
Died 1779, 'of Killua', being succeeded by his son BENJAMIN.

The *Eton College Lists* also shows an unidentifiable Chapman as being in the Sixth Form on 2 November 1728; with another (possibly a Colleger) in the 'II' Form in 1742, and in the Fourth Form in 1745.

BENJAMIN CHAPMAN: c.1745-1810.

Born c.1745, eldest son of BENJAMIN CHAPMAN (c.1700-1779) above.
Attended the Rev. Charles Meares School at Lackan, co. Westmeath.
11 November 1761 entered Trinity College, Dublin as a Pensioner.
1763-1775 On the Grand Jury for co. Westmeath.
1768 Michaelmas, became a barrister in Dublin.

According to a letter dated 11 March 1837, from Sir Thomas Benjamin's agent to Lieutenant Wynne, 'The town of Clonmellon was first commenced by the late Sir Benjamin Chapman about between 60-70 years ago [c.1770]. It got its name from a moat near the town called Cruckmillion.'
1772. Doctor of Law (*"honoris causa"*) at Dublin.
1772-1776 M.P. for the Borough of Fore in Irish Parliament.
1776-1783 M.P. for co. Westmeath.
Married by licence dated 20 February 1776 to Anne, the only child of John Lowther of Staffordstown, co. Meath (by Anne née Billing), and died c.1801.

Amongst the National Portrait Gallery's photographic collection is a copy of *The Irish House of Commons* by Francis Wheatley (in private hands), signed and dated 1780. One of the figures portrayed is that of 'Sir Bej[n] Chapman'. Unlike some other persons there he is not further designated as "Bart" in the *Key to the Picture*. Thus there is a possibility that he may have earlier been knighted. According to this portrait he had a narrow face, with a simple wig.

In February/March 1782 was created a Baronet of Ireland, with remainder in default of male issue, to the male descendants of his father. The Chapman Arms: *Per chevron, argent and gules, in the centre, a crescent counter-charged.* Crest: *An arm, embowed, in armour, holding a broken spear, encircled with a wreath of laurel all proper.* Motto: *Crescit sub pondere virtus.* (Virtue thrives under oppression).
c.1784 saw the building of Killua House - see below. Killua is thought to have been derived from the Irish 'Killaloo' =

the church of Do Lua.
1795-1809 Sir Benjamin on the Grand Jury of Westmeath.

Jacky Dalton, the land steward to Sir Benjamin in the late 18th century had a close relationship with his employer, and would sit at the foot of Sir Benjamin's dinner table wearing a particularly strange yellow wig and playing bagpipes for guests. He is believed to have relieved his master of considerable sums of money, but after his master's death turned to drink, and finally committed suicide by jumping into one of the many lakes on the estate.

Probably during the Irish Insurrection of 1798 Sir Benjamin (as recalled later to his correspondent, Lord Shelburne), he had gone to a cold dinner at a friend's house some five miles from Trim, co. Meath:

What a dessert had we to our frugal repast! The sudden and shocking exhibition from our windows of the perspective of a conflagration of the surrounding mansions, of farmers and peasants flying for shelter in all directions and unexpectedly involved in this dreadful calamity; a regiment of Scotch Fencibles enjoyed this savage triumph and fired upon the fugitives while thirty wretched houses...with every sort of provision, rustic furniture and implements of husbandry were all consumed by the merciless flames before our eyes. I could hear no reason save that a robbery had been attempted without success a few days before on a gentleman in that vicinage.

Sir BENJAMIN died in July/August 1810, without issue

at an advanced age [c.65], at his seat at St. Lucy

being succeeded by his brother THOMAS (1756-1837), and his will was proved the same year.

This first Killua House was a large 3-storey house of around 1784. What preceded this as the Chapman home is not known, though it has been said by Ryan-Smolin that the old family home, St. Lucy's, was pulled down at the same time. It had a curved bow in the centre of one front, and a 3-sided bow in the centre of the other. It had a Georgian symmetry, as well as Georgian sash-windows. The entrance door opened into an octagon hall with delicate late 18th century plasterwork in lunettes over the doors. Beyond the hall was a round room in the middle of the garden front.

William Sadler II (c.1782-1839) painted three views of Killua, between 1812-1821. The first was of the original Killua house from across the lake. He also painted another view across the lake, this time towards the distant gothic ruins of the church on a hillside inside the family graveyard; whilst in the middle distance there are sham ruins made from stones brought in from an old abbey by Sir Benjamin in 1800, forming an entrance to that part of the garden in which the holy well of St. Lucy is situated. A third painting was across the park of Killua, taken from the entrance front of the house, with the spire of Clonmellon Church in the distance. The natural lake was first enlarged in the 1790s, and then further increased in 1812 and 1818.

In his *Topography of Ireland* Lewis says:

The church of St. Lucy, which is at Clonmellon, and is a neat structure with a handsome spire, was built [c.1780], partly at the expense of Sir Benjamin Chapman...Here [at Killua] is an almshouse for four poor women, who have a weekly allowance from the Chapman family; and in Clonmellon are ten almshouses for aged and infirm labourers, who have each more than an acre of land, and £2 per annum, £5 being appropriated for keeping the houses in repair: they were established under the will of Sir Benjamin Chapman...There are some remains of the old church, with a burial ground attached, which is the place of internment of the Chapman family.

THOMAS CHAPMAN: (1756-1837)

Born 20 October 1756, the second son of BENJAMIN CHAPMAN (c.1700-1779) above.

Educated at Rev. Charles Meares' school at Lackan, co. Westmeath.

Entered Trinity College, Dublin, as a Pensioner, on 8 July 1774, aged 18.

December 1780 was knighted in Ireland.

1808 married Margaret Anne, second daughter of James Fetherstonhaugh, of Bracklyn Castle, co. Westmeath, (by Margaret, daughter of Sir Richard Steele, 1st baronet), who died at Killua Castle 21 January 1871, aged 83, having three sons:

MONTAGUE LOWTHER (1808-1853) 3rd Baronet: see below;
BENJAMIN JAMES (1810-1888) 4th Baronet: see below;
WILLIAM (1812-1889): see below.

1810 succeeded his brother BENJAMIN junior above as 2nd baronet.

1834 believed date of erection of the Ralegh obelisk on Killua estate.

On the Grand Jury of Westmeath 1811-1825.

Had a residence at 34 Merrion Square, Dublin (according to the 1839 *Almanack & Directory*.)

He died in 23 December 1837, aged 81, being succeeded by his eldest son MONTAGUE LOWTHER CHAPMAN.

Lewis's *Topography of Ireland* notes:

Killua Castle is the handsome castellated residence of Sir T. Chapman, Bart., and contains a fine collection of paintings by the old masters; the demesne comprises more than 500 acres, and includes a sheet of water, an obelisk to Sir Walter Raleigh, and the ruins of a commandery of the Knights of St. John of Jerusalem...The parochial school [at Clonmellon], which is under the National Board, but was built by Sir Thomas Chapman...

The castellation of Killua House was apparently done in the 1820s and 1830s. The additions included battlements, a round tower (1821), and two polygonal towers, and refacing it with random ashlar. This remodelling has been attributed to James Shiel, who did similar work nearby. A single-storey castellated wing was also added at one side; but on the whole the house kept its Georgian symmetry, as well as many of its Georgian sash-windows. The entrance door in the 3-sided bow kept its semi-circular fanlight, while being given a suitably Gothic surround. It became a large and romantic demesne, with its now two lakes, and follies. An obelisk to Lord Nelson was erected in 1806/7. There was also the erection in 1834 of an obelisk, commemorating the alleged planting by Sir Walter Raleigh of the first potato in Ireland.

Around the perimeter of the estate are dotted five gate lodges.

1. The Palladian-style Temple Lodge of 1804/7, (and still lived in). At the front, at the apex of the roof there is a little platform on which used to stand a small statue of the Angel Gabriel; and at the base of the roof there is a projection on each side on which there used to be small statues of ordinary angels. This lodge is on the opposite side of the road to the drive entrance - the gate of which was left unoiled, and thus the squeaking of the gate gave warning to the lodge keepers.

2. The Clonmellon Lodge of the same date, but transformed into a triple-towered Gothic folly c.1828 (and also still lived in).

3. Whilst at this latter date was built the Gothic Lodge, the only one with an arch for vehicles.

4-5. Two others in 1855 and 1856 on the Kells road approaches to the Castle.

Near to the Palladium Lodge driveway there is an old Ice-house, which used to be filled with ice from the estate's lake.

There is an unresolved record of a Benjamin Chapman, son of Sir Thomas Chapman, co. Westmeath, who entered Trinity College, Dublin, on 25 May 1795, aged 17, as a *socius comitatus*. Had been to the school of the Rev. William Darby of Ballygall, co. Dublin.

A *socius comitatus* was a Fellow Commoner who paid double fees and enjoyed certain privileges, including that of finishing the College course in three years instead of four. He would thus have come from a wealthy family.

MONTAGUE LOWTHER CHAPMAN (1808-1853)

Born 10 December 1808, eldest son of THOMAS CHAPMAN (1756-1837) above.

Entered Trinity College, Dublin, on 18 October 1824, aged 15, as a *socius comitatus*, having had a prior private tutor. Obtained a B.A. in 1828.

1830-1841 M.P. for co. Westmeath for five Irish Parliaments.

On the Grand Jury for Westmeath 1830-1834, 1838-1849.

1837 succeeded his father THOMAS CHAPMAN above as 3rd baronet.

1844 served as High Sheriff of co. Westmeath.

17 May 1853 died in a drowning accident at sea, near Australia, aged 44. According to an unidentified newspaper report (probably Irish), he was said to have owned a lot of land in Australia, and brought many people over from the Clonmellon area.

Being unmarried he was succeeded by his brother BENJAMIN JAMES.

BENJAMIN JAMES CHAPMAN (1810-1888)

Born 9 February 1810, at Killua, the second son of THOMAS CHAPMAN (1756-1837) above.
19 October 1824 entered Trinity College, Dublin, aged 14, as a *socius comitatus* (having had a prior private tutor), with B.A. in 1830.
On the Grand Jury for Westmeath 1831-1845.
Barrister at Dublin, Michaelmas 1835.
1841-1847 M.P. for co. Westmeath in Irish Parliament, from his elder brother Montague.
1853 succeeded his brother MONTAGUE LOWTHER above as 4th baronet.
Married 22 July 1849 to Maria Sarah Fetherstonhaugh, first daughter of his maternal uncle, Richard Steele Fetherstonhaugh of Rockview, co. Westmeath (by Dorothea, daughter of Denis George, 1st Baronet). She died 9 October 1898 at Bray, being buried in Killua cemetery where there is a headstone. Benjamin and Maria had two sons and two daughters:

MONTAGUE RICHARD (1853-1907): see below;
BENJAMIN RUPERT (1865-1914): see below.
Dora Marguerite: Born c.1850 at Killua. Died 19 November 1921, and buried in Killua cemetery, where there is a headstone.
Maria: Born c.1850. Died 19 October 1898, and buried in Killua cemetery, where there is a headstone.

1856 Sheriff of co. Westmeath.
He was said to have travelled extensively in Europe, and collected a lot of fine furniture and paintings.
There was a photograph taken of the Westmeath Hunt, showing a mounted Sir Benjamin.
In 1878 the family estates consisted of 9,516 acres in co. Westmeath (gross annual value £6,532), 3,600 acres in co. Mayo (valued at only around £50 a year), and 241 acres in co. Meath (at £217). Total: 13,357 acres, worth £6,799 a year.
28 March 1883 Lord Lieutenant and Custos Rotulorum of co. Westmeath until his death.
A member of the Reform Club, in Kildare Street, Dublin.

There is a photograph of Sir Benjamin and Lady Chapman in a horse-drawn carriage in front of the impressive studded front door of Killua Castle, possibly taken not long before his death.

Sir BENJAMIN died 3 November 1888, at the Shelburne Hotel in Dublin, in his 79th year, being succeeded by his son MONTAGUE RICHARD (1853-1907). His widow died 9 October 1898, at Bray.

His will was proved 11 February 1889 at Mullingar, co. Westmeath, by his son Sir Montague Chapman (1853-1907), of Killua Castle, one of the Executors. Value of effects £26,071.13s.5d.

MONTAGUE RICHARD CHAPMAN (1853-1907)

Born 22 February 1853, in Dublin, eldest son of BENJAMIN JAMES CHAPMAN (1810-1888) above.
23 May 1872 matriculated at Christ Church, Oxford, aged 19. Obtained a B.A. in 1875.
1876-1881 Master of the Westmeath Hunt. 'As Killua is in the extreme north-east corner of Westmeath, on a point jutting into co. Meath, and in Meath hunting country, he could not work things from home, and so took rooms in Mullingar for the hunting season. He was thus on the spot to direct operations, and look after the many details of the Hunt establishment. He was a big man, riding over fourteen stone, always usefully mounted and generally in the first flight, taking more note of his hounds than did some of the scatter-brained thrusters in front of him.' Amongst the Hunt's Stewards were his father Sir Benjamin, and Francis Chapman. He instituted Point-to-Point Races in Westmeath.
A J.P.
1888 succeeded his father BENJAMIN JAMES (1810-1888) as 5th baronet.
Was sometime a Captain in the 9th Battalion of the Rifle Brigade (Militia).
1889 Sheriff of co. Westmeath.
9 January 1894 married his cousin, Caroline Margaret, only daughter of his paternal uncle, William Chapman, of South Hill, Delvin, co. Westmeath (by Louisa, daughter of Col. Arthur Vansittart of Shottesbrooke Park, Berks). They did not have any children. Caroline died 8 December 1919, being buried in Killua cemetery, where there is a headstone.
The accompanying photograph of Sir Montague appeared in *Records of the Westmeath Hunt* by Edmund Dease, 1898.
Died 23 January 1907, and buried in Killua cemetery, where there is a headstone; being succeeded by his brother BENJAMIN RUPERT as 6th baronet.

This branch of the family from which T. E. Lawrence was descended acquired in due course the large manor house of South Hill, near the village of Delvin.

After Sir Montague's widow's death in 1919, having lived the rest of her life at Killua Castle, this latter Chapman manor house was sold, and later dismantled. In the *Westmeath Examiner* of Saturday, 29 May 1920, an advertisement was carried announcing the auction of the contents of the house. The inventory of paintings offered for sale included works by Rembrandt, Rubens, and other great Italian and Dutch artists.

Killua Castle was inherited by a cousin, General Fetherstonhaugh, related by marriage to the Chapmans; being then sold to a succession of owners, one of whom held a sale of its fittings in 1944, which must have been just after the last Hunt Ball said to have been held there. Shortly afterwards the roof was removed, and its lead sold to a firm of builders' providers in Dublin.

The Fetherstonhaughs married into the Frampton family of Moreton in Dorset, England, who were owners of the cottage at nearby Clouds Hill which T. E. Lawrence was to buy as his home.

When Killua Castle was visited by the author in June 2000, the still spectacular building was an abandoned, ruinous, derelict, vandalised, graffiti marked shell. This however made it possible to view traces of the brickwork of the original house before its castellation. The older part faces the Ralegh obelisk. At the inside corners of both towers each side of the main doorway is a stone embedded into the ground to deflect coach wheels from hitting the towers themselves. Within the small octagonal entrance hall were several open entrances to cellars, with steps down having been deliberately destroyed to stop access. Over doorways leading from this hallway were still traces of decorated plasterwork. To the left was what was believed to have been the ballroom, with a larger room (in the newer 1860s extension) leading off, both with a rear view through over the grounds to the south. From the cellar under this latter room could be seen the entrance to a tunnel leading from the house, but of which the exit is not known. On the outer wall of the extension facing the park there can still be seen niches which used to contain dummy windows complete with frames and glass. Well established trees and bushes are growing inside the building, which are hastening its ultimate destruction.

Outside, abutting onto the end of the extension is a sunken cattle pen, reached through a pillared entrance by a narrow sunken track cut into the hillside, which can be crossed by what remains of a small iron bridge.

The pleasure gardens, labyrinth and woods have long disappeared, though the lines of the various drives which used to be tree-lined can be discerned. The lakes are now but bogs. There apparently used to be a cottage in the estate woods, where the Chapmen men did their love-making with the females of the district; and whose names appeared on birth certificates as father.

Deteriorating are the Gothic Lodge, which has a top corner broken by a falling tree, and the 18th century brick built ice-house, near to the family cemetery in which very little remains of the old church. On the road running along the western side of the estate there is a house and what used to be the kennels. In the river nearby there was a ram which used to pump water up to the lakes. South of the road running to the south of the estate there used to be the deer park. The Killua cemetery is situated along this road. A small metal fenced plot contains four headstones, whilst an earlier slab is higher up. Very little of the church now remains.

The Ralegh obelisk was showing some signs of neglect, with stones falling out of one corner, and bushes growing out of it. On one of its tablets someone at some time had obviously carved an additional initial 'G' in Ralegh's name, for what reason is not known, so that it now reads:

TO THE MEMORY
OF
SIR WALTER
GRALEIGH

The other tablet reads: 'Erected By Sir Thomas Chapman Bar^{t} AD 1810'. This date must refer to his being granted his baronetcy.

Wherever one travels around the outside of the estate, Killua Castle is generally visible up on its eminence. Conversely, more or less the whole estate is visible from the Castle, especially by anyone standing on the roof as used to be possible.

Killua Castle, together with five acres of land was said to be for sale at Ir£300,000.

At the craft-shop tea-room in Clonmellon's wide main street, on the building's outside wall, there is a carved stone showing a bent arm holding an arrow, obviously taken from the Chapman crest, with the date 'AD 1835'. This had been found in a cottage between Clonmellon and Athboy.

BENJAMIN RUPERT CHAPMAN (1865-1914)

Born 7 December 1865 at Killua Castle, second son of BENJAMIN JAMES CHAPMAN (1810 1888) above.
Married. Did not have any children.
22 January 1907 succeeded his brother MONTAGUE (1853-1907) as the 6th baronet.
A photograph was taken c.1900, of Sir Benjamin in cricket clothes and holding a bat, in a group of five other players, and scorer.
Died 24 March 1914, and buried in Killua cemetery, where there is a headstone; being succeeded by his cousin THOMAS ROBERT TIGHE CHAPMAN (1846-1919) as 7th (and last) baronet.

WILLIAM CHAPMAN (1811-1889)

Born 4 November 1811, at Killua, co. Westmeath, third son of Sir THOMAS CHAPMAN (1756-1837) above.
Entered Trinity College, Dublin, on 22 October 1827, aged 15, as a *socius comitatus*, after having had a prior private tutor. Obtained a B.A. in 1831.
1835 on Grand Jury of co. Westmeath.
4 August 1841 married Louisa, third daughter of Col. Arthur Vansittart of Shottesbrooke Park, Berks, by Hon. Caroline Eden his wife, dau. of William Eden, 1st Baron Auckland (1744-1814), whose wife Eleanor Elliott was a sister of the 1st Earl of Minto; and also niece of Lord Bexley. Caroline died 13 March 1877 at Killua. She and William had three sons and a daughter:

William Eden: Born 4 August 1844 at South Hill, Delvin, educated at Eton, a major in the 15th Hussars, died 6 May 1870.

THOMAS ROBERT TIGHE CHAPMAN (1846-1919): see below, as 7th Baronet.

Caroline Margaret: Born c.1848 at South Hill, Delvin; c.1875 married her cousin MONTAGUE CHAPMAN the 5th baronet; she used to keep in touch with her ostracised brother THOMAS; was to be ill for several years; a codicil to her Will dated June 1916 she had to sign with an "X" and witnessed by two nurses; she died 8 December 1919, and was buried in Killua cemetery, where there is a headstone.

Francis Vansittart: Born 9 September 1849 at South Hill, Delvin; educated at Eton; on death of his father in 1840 he was trained to run the family estates; J.P. for co. Westmeath; has been said to have liked his whiskey; 1915 died unmarried.

WILLIAM was said to have enjoyed considerable wealth and social standing, and becoming High Sheriff of co. Westmeath. Also Deputy Lieutenant and a J.P.
When living at South Hill, Delvin, co. Westmeath he was shown as being of the Reform Club, Kildare Street, Dublin; and having an estate of 5,042 acres in co. Westmeath (annual value £3,398), 1,386 acres in co. Meath (£1,217),

and 2,664 acres in co. Mayo (£88) - totalling 9,092 acres (£4,703 value).
Though in 1878 the family estates were said to consist of 9,516 acres in co. Westmeath, 3,600 acres in co. Mayo (valued at only £36 a year), and 241 acres in co. Meath. Total: 13,357 acres, worth £6,785 a year.
He died 28 January 1889 at South Hill. His will (with one codicil) was proved at Mullingar, co. Westmeath, by his son Francis Vansittart Chapman, Esq. of South Hill, one of the Executors. Effects valued at £22,466 12s. 4d.

South Hill was originally a plain 3-storey, 7-bay, early 19th century house, with interior plasterwork of the Morrison school. It passed by inheritance from a branch of the Tighe family to the Chapmans.

THOMAS ROBERT TIGHE CHAPMAN (aka LAWRENCE) (1846-1919)

Born 6 November 1846, at South Hill, Delvin, co. Westmeath, second son of WILLIAM CHAPMAN (1811-1889) above.
Had a sound classical schooling at Eton (when his early known photograph was probably taken). In co. Westmeath Central Library at Mullingar is a photocopy of the following:

Thomas R. T. Chapman
With the kind wishes
of Harry S. C. Everard
his schoolfellow.
===========
On his leaving Eton Coll:
Christmas : 1865

He then took an agricultural course. There were some years of continental travel and mountaineering.
In 1870, on death of his elder brother, William, he took over management of the estate. He lived on his private means, which permitted of comfort, but not luxury. He became keenly interested in church architecture and in photography. He was also an enthusiastic yachtsman, shot, and in due course - with the introduction of the safety bicycle - a cyclist.
24 July 1873 he married Edith Sarah Hamilton, daughter of George Augustus Rochfort Boyd of Middleton Park, Castletown-Geoghegan, co. Westmeath. Whilst living at Clanhugh, near Mullingar, they had four daughters - Eva Jane Louisa (1874-), Rose Isabel (1878-), Florence Lina (1880-1996), and Mabel Cecile (1882-1941?), all of whom remained unmarried. Whilst still living at South Hill, Edith died October 1930.
At some stage he became a J.P.
In 1885 he ran away with the family governess, Sarah Junner/Maden, and they subsequently had five sons:

Montague Robert, born December 1885, Dublin, Ireland, though no trace found in 1999 at The General Register Office in Dublin.

THOMAS EDWARD (Lawrence of Arabia), born 16 August 1888, Tremadog, N.Wales, with no local baptism record able to be found.

William George, born 1889, Kirkcudbright, Scotland, with no local baptism record able to be found.

Frank Helier, born 1893, Jersey, C.I.

Arnold Walter, born 1900, Oxford.

On 7 December 1914 he succeeded his cousin BENJAMIN RUPERT CHAPMAN (1865-1914) as 7th baronet.
Sir THOMAS died 9 April 1919 (during the general flu epidemic) at 2 Polstead Road, Oxford; and was buried in the Wolvecote Cemetery, in the north of Oxford, where there are memorials to himself and other family members. Since none of his illegitimate sons could of course inherit the title, and there presumably not being any other family claimants, with his death the baronetcy became extinct.

South Hill was sold in the 1950s, and bought by the Sisters of Charity of Jesus and Mary, who extended and converted it into a hospital and school for mentally handicapped children.

Like the other members of the displaced Protestant gentry of English origins, the Chapmans looked to England for help, married into their own group, mingled little if at all with the surrounding Irish Catholic peasantry (who regarded them with suspicion and resentment), and satisfied their sense of social responsibility by doing good works of the Lady Bountiful variety in the local community. As one Irish schoolteacher of Delvin said, the "planters" were "not Irish", did not look after their tenants who worked the farms, "grabbed" land from the people, and gave little in return.

RECAPITULATION

In Chapter 1 it was considered that there were seven separate but connected aspects that had to be researched, in order to determine as far as possible the various truths about the perceived Chapman-Ralegh-Lawrence connection, etc.:

1. *That a Chapman family, possibly from the Hinckley area of Leicestershire were related to the famous 16/17th century Devonian - Sir Walter Ralegh.*

There is reasonable evidence now to confidently be of the opinion that the Chapman family of 16th century Ireland was derived from the Champernowne family of Devon. In Chapter 2 it was seen that during the 1400s and 1500s Champernownes from Modbury married into land-owning families of Leicestershire, and so acquired properties there - the so-called Hinckley aspect. These same Champernownes were to become related to Sir Walter Ralegh through his father and great-grandfather both marrying into that family. *Debrett's* original supposition thus seems to have been correct after all, as was the original 1828 *Burke's Peerage and Baronetage* statement of a <u>maternal</u> cousin-german connection mentioned in Chapter 1.

There also seems to be fairly conclusive proof that the then contemporary names of Champen, Champion, Chapman, etc. were all corruptions of Champernowne - which itself had previously successively been Chambernon, Champernon, and Champernoun.

2. *That the brothers John and William Chapman from this family obtained lands in Munster.*

Ample documented proof has been found of a John Champen/Champion being granted lands in co. Kerry, Munster, Ireland in the 1580s. And although there has not been found any conclusive proof that this same John (and his supposed brother William) were members of the Champernowne/Chapman family, there was the Charles Smith quote in 1756 of 15/16th century Fynes Moryson saying that John Champion was also known as John Chapman. It is known for certainty that some members of the Champernowne family were in Ireland during the late 1500s, and at least one was killed there - a George Chapman/Champernowne in 1581 coincidentally at about the same time as a George Chapman.

This study is thus now in the realm of mathematical probability by means of best possible fit, in believing that a Ralegh kinsman had land grants in Munster. It has, alas, not been possible to substantiate that John had a brother William.

3. *That this [grant] was through their connection with their alleged kinsman.*

Other than the possibility that John Chapman fought alongside his cousin Walter Ralegh in Ireland, and Sir William Herbert's later observation that John Champion was "a Ralegh man", there has not been found any evidence that Ralegh was directly influential in John obtaining his Munster lands. They both had mutual family connections in 'high places', such that Ralegh's direct intervention may not have been needed. The main criteria for obtaining such plantation lands would appear to have been money and commitment, and there is no evidence that the Champernownes lacked either.

4. *What and where these lands were in Munster.*

Again there has been found ample contemporary documentation of these lands, several of which the author has been able to visit. As well as sources listing and describing properties, there was the 1589 map (illustrated) showing the name of 'CHAMPYON' (with that of his joint-grantee STONE) inserted in the appropriate area.

5. *That these same lands were sold subsequently to the 1st Earl of Cork, and the circumstances of such.*

Yet again there have been found many contemporary documents confirming the sale, but not as yet (by the author) anything seen confirming the alleged sale price of £26,400.

6. *That there is a provable, or at least reasonably acceptable, unbroken genealogical line from these first Chapman settlers in Ireland down to T. E. Lawrence.*

This has not been possible. There is a clear line from the 17th century captain Benjamin Chapman of co. Westmeath, right up to T. E. Lawrence; but only supposition can relate the original John (and William) to this same Benjamin. It is possible that the latter was a grandson of one of the former, but it is highly unlikely now that this can ever be substantiated beyond reasonable doubt. There are, however, one or two tantilising possible missing-links, e.g. the Thomas Champion, High Sheriff of Westmeath in 1607.

7. *How the subsequent Chapman family fared generally over the centuries, down to the time of T. E. Lawrence, including acquisition of further land and property, and any later disposal.*

The Champernowne/Chapman generations consistently increased the sizes of their estates by judicious marriages with heiresses. But conversely they also lost properties with their own daughters' dowers. Even more debilitating was the continual lack - for various reasons - of male heirs, which meant that the family properties became so concentrated in one Chapman line that eventually ended at Killua, and resulted in its sale in the 1920s; and another at South Hill with four unmarried daughters, and subsequent five illegitimate sons, that it too had to be sold in the 1950s.

In spite of local rumours, there is no evidence that T.E.Lawrence ever visited Ireland.

On 27 January 1924, whilst he was stationed at Bovington Camp, in Dorset, Lawrence wrote to Mrs Florence Hardy, the wife of the Dorset novelist and poet Thomas Hardy, who lived at Max Gate on the outskirts of Dorchester only a few miles away. He often used to visit them on his series of Brough motorcycles.

I think you came here [his cottage Clouds Hill] yesterday: - ...But that picture of Killua , , , , surely that was Frampton property. Am I to think of it as a gift (once I meant to earn money & buy the place; now I'm wiser & want only to buy Clouds' Hill...If it's a gift, then please who's gift - for I'd owe a letter of thanks. Will you be good enough to enlighten my darkness?

Although Florence's reply is not known, the picture had probably come from the Fetherstonhaugh-Frampton family at Moreton, Dorset, with whom she was friendly. A branch of the Fetherstonhaugh family had been settled in co. Westmeath for several generations, and had married twice into the Chapman family there in 1808 and 1849, and once into the Frampton family of Moreton in 1855. The Fetherstonhaugh-Framptons had therefore been well placed to inherit Killua in the 1920s, but then promptly sold it.

In March 1927 Lawrence wrote to Charlotte Shaw, wife of George Bernard Shaw, that he would like to buy some acres of land in the Irish county from which his father had come, in order 'to keep some of Walter Raleigh's gift in the family'.

In a letter to Edward Garnett, on 27 August 1924, Lawrence mentioned his father's resemblance to Ralegh who wasn't an ancestor, only the son of one. Which as was seen in Chapter 1 was not strictly true.

Other than finding a firm direct line from John and William Chapman of Kerry to captain Benjamin Chapman of Westmeath, the other remaining mystery is from whence all those original submitted details came from.

BIBLIOGRAPHY

Aldington, Richard *Lawrence of Arabia* Collins 1955

l'Anson, Bryan *The History of Chapman Family, Vol. 1.* 1917

Austen-Leigh, R.A. (Ed.) *Eton College Lists 1678-1790* Spottiswoode & Co. 1907

Baring-Gould, S. (Rev.) & Twigge, R. *An Armory of the Western Counties [c.1550]* James G. Commins 1898

Bartlett, Thomas & Jeffery, Keith (ed.) *A Military History of Ireland* CUP 1996

Bary, Valerie *Houses of Kerry* Ballinakella Press, Whitegate, co.Clare 1994

Bateman, John *The Great Landowners of Great Britain and Ireland* Harrison, London 1883

Beddow, Rev. Arthur J.C. *A History of Bere Ferrers Parish* 1995

Bence-Jones, Mark *Burke's guide to Country Houses, Vol. 1 - Ireland* Burke's Peerage Ltd 1978

Bence-Jones, Mark *A Guide to Irish Country Houses* Constable 1988

Book of Surveys and Distribution of the Estates of the County of Westmeath Forfeited in the Year 1641 Ladiston 1852

Bridger, Charles *Index To Printed Pedigrees Contained In County & Local Histories, Etc.* London 1867

Burke, John *The Commoners of Great Britain and Ireland, Vol. II* Henry Colburn 1835

Burke *The General Armory of England, Scotland, Ireland and Wales* 1884

Burke *Landed Gentry* Various editions

Burtchaell, George Dames & Sadler, Thomas Ulick (Eds.) *Alumni Dublinenses 1593-1846* Williams & Norgate 1924

Butler, W.F.T. *Gleanings from Irish History* 1925

Catalogue of Graduates in University of Dublin, A Hodges, Smith, and Foster Dublin 1869

Census of Ireland for Year of 1851

Census of Ireland 1901: General Topographical Index HMSO 1904

Champernowne, C.E. *The Champernowne Family* Private 1953

Chapman, Alan *Corespondence*

Chapman, Clifford *Correspondence*
Chapman, Steve *Correspondence*
Cokayne, George Edward *The Complete Baronetage* Alan Sutton 1983
Craig, Maurice and the Knight of Glin *Ireland Observed* Mercier Press, Cork 1970
Cuppage, Judith, et al *Corca Dhuibhne - Dingle Peninsula Archaeological Survey* Ballyferriter 1986
Dictionary of National Biography
Dease, Edmund *Records of the Westmeath Hunt* 1898
Ellis, Peter Berresford *Hell or Connaught! The Cromwellian Colonisation of Ireland 1652-1660* The Blackstaff Press 1989
Foley, Patrick *History of the County Kerry-Corkaguiney* Dublin 1907
Foster, R.F. *Modern Ireland 1600-1972* Penguin 1989
Friends of St. Andrew's, Bere Ferrers *Church Guide* 1996
Glin, Knight of, et al *Vanishing Country Houses of Ireland* Irish Georgian Society 1988
Grosart, Rev. Alexander B. *The Lismore Papers (First Series)* Privately Published 1886
Harbison, Peter *Guide to National and Historic Monuments of Ireland* Gill & Macmillan, Dublin 1992
Hickson, Mary Agnes *Selections from Old Kerry Records* Watson & Hazell, London 1872
Hickson, Mary Agnes *Selections from Old Kerry Records, Second Selection* Watson & Hazell, London 1874
Kerry Magazine, The Tralee 1 September 1854
Hitchcock, Richard 'Dingle In The Sixteenth Century' *Journal of the Royal Society of Arts of Ireland, Vol. 2.* 1852
Hore, Philip Herbert (ed.) *History of the Town and County of Wexford. Old and New Ross* Eliot Stock, London 1900
Index to the Townlands and Towns, Parishes and Baronies of Ireland Genealogical Publishing Co. Inc, Baltimore 1984
King, Jeremiah *County Kerry Past and Present* The Mercier Press, Dublin 1986
King, J. & E. *King's Irish-English Dictionary* The Mercier Press, Dublin 1986

King, J. *History of Kerry, or history of the parishes in the County* Liverpool n.d.
Knightly, Phillip & Simpson, Colin *The Secret Lives of Lawrence of Arabia* Nelson 1969
Lacey, Robert *Sir Walter Ralegh* Sphere Books 1975
Lewis, Samuel *A Topographical Dictionary of England, Vols 1-4* S.Lewis & Co., London 1844
Lewis, Samuel *A Topographical Dictionary of Ireland Vol.1 A-J 2nd Edn* S.Lewis & Co., London 1846
Lewis, Samuel *A Topographical Dictionary of Ireland Vol.2 K-Z 2nd Edn* S.Lewis & Co., London 1847
Lewis, Samuel *A Topographical Dictionary of Ireland Atlas* S.Lewis & Co., London 1846
Loyd, L.C. *The Origins of some Anglo-Norman Families* Harleian Society 1951
MacCarthy-Morrogh, Michael *The Munster Plantation 1583-1641* Ph.D. Thesis Oxford University 1983
MacCarthy-Morrogh, Michael *The Munster Plantation: English Migration to Southern Ireland 1583-1641* OUP 1986
MacLyacht, Edward *Irish Families: Their Names, Arms & Origins* Helicon Ltd, Dublin 1957
MacLyacht, Edward *The Surnames of Ireland* Irish Academic Press, co. Dublin 1989
Marshall, David *Best walks in Ireland* Constable 1996
Maxwell, Constantia *Irish History From Contemporary Sources (1509-1610)* Allen & Unwin 1923
McKee. Alexander *From Merciless Invaders* Souvenir Press 1987
McMorran, R. & C. *Dingle: A Guide Book* 1980
Mee, Arthur (ed.) *Devon* Hodder & Stoughton 1938
Mee, Arthur (ed.) *Leicestershire* Hodder & Stoughton 1937
Modbury Local History Society *The Parish Church of St. George, Modbury, South Devon* 1998
Nichols, John *The History & Antiquities of Leicestershire 1795-1807*
O'Donovan, John, et al *Ordnance Survey Letters of 1841* Bray 1927
O'Hart, John *The Irish and Anglo-Irish Landed Gentry when Cromwell came to Ireland* Irish University Press 1969

Ordnance Survey of Ireland *Discovery Series of Maps, 1:50,000. Nos. 63, 70, and 71* 1995

Peacock, Edward (ed.) *The Army Lists of the Roundheads and Cavaliers of 1642* John Camden Hatton, London 1863

Pender, Séamus *A Census of Ireland c.1659* Stationery Office, Dublin 1939

Polwhele, Rev. Richard *The History of Devon, Volume 3* Kohler & Coombes 1977

Power, Denis, et al *Archaeological Inventory of County Cork, Vols. I-III* Staionery Office, Dublin 1992

Prendergast, John. P. *The Cromwellian Settlement of Ireland* Constable 1996

Public Record Office *Calendar of State Papers (Ireland)* SP/63 series

Ranger, T.O. *The Career of Richard Boyle, First Earl of Cork in Ireland 1588-1643* Ph.D. Thesis Oxford University 1959

Reilly, Tom *Cromwell: An Honourable Enemy* Mount Eagle Publications Ltd, Dingle, Co. Kerry, Ireland 1999

Rose-Troup, Frances *The Western Rebellion of 1549* Smith, Elder & Co., London 1913

Ryan-Smolin, Wanda 'William Sadler's Views of Killua Castle, C. Westmeath' *Irish Arts Review, Vol. 12* 1996

Sandford, Michael J.G. *A History of The Ralegh Family of Fardel & Budleigh in the Early Tudor Period* M.A. Thesis. University of London 1955

Sheehy, Maurice *Walks of Discovery in the Dingle Peninsula* 1982

Smith, Charles *Antient and Present State of the County of Kerry* 1750

The Kerryman August-November 1927 at NLI

Traill, H.D. & Mann, J.S. (Eds.) *Social England, Vol III 1509-1603* Cassell 1903

Tuckett, John *Devonshire Pedigrees, Heralds' Visitations 1620, plus the Printed Collection of Westcote and Pole* Westcountry Studies Library, Exeter

Waldman, Milton *Sir Walter Raleigh* Collins 1950

Walsh, Rev. Paul *The Placenames of Westmeath* Dublin Institute for Advanced Studies 1957

Wilson, Jeremy *Lawrence of Arabia* Heinemann 1989